THIRD EDITION

PowerShell Pocket Reference
Portable Help for PowerShell Scripters

Lee Holmes

Beijing · Boston · Farnham · Sebastopol · Tokyo

PowerShell Pocket Reference

by Lee Holmes

Published by O'Reilly Media, Inc., 1005 Gravenstein Highway North, Sebastopol, CA 95472.

O'Reilly books may be purchased for educational, business, or sales promotional use. Online editions are also available for most titles (*http://oreilly.com*). For more information, contact our corporate/institutional sales department: 800-998-9938 or *corporate@oreilly.com*.

Acquisitions Editor: Suzanne McQuade
Development Editor: Angela Rufino
Production Editor: Kate Galloway
Copyeditor: Stephanie English
Proofreader: Jasmine Kwityn
Indexer: Potomac Indexing, LLC
Interior Designer: David Futato
Cover Designer: Karen Montgomery
Illustrator: Kate Dullea

May 2021:   Third Edition

Revision History for the Third Edition

2021-04-22:   First Release

See   *http://oreilly.com/catalog/errata.csp?isbn=9781098101671*   for   release details.

978-1-098-10167-1

[LSI]

Table of Contents

A Guided Tour of PowerShell

Introduction

PowerShell has revolutionized the world of system management and command-line shells. From its object-based pipelines to its administrator focus to its enormous reach into other Microsoft management technologies, PowerShell drastically improves the productivity of administrators and power users alike.

When you're learning a new technology, it's natural to feel bewildered at first by all the unfamiliar features and functionality. This perhaps rings especially true for users new to PowerShell because it may be their first experience with a fully featured command-line shell. Or worse, they've heard stories of PowerShell's fantastic integrated scripting capabilities and fear being forced into a world of programming that they've actively avoided until now.

Fortunately, these fears are entirely misguided; PowerShell is a shell that both grows with you and grows on you. Let's take a tour to see what it is capable of:

- PowerShell works with standard Windows commands and applications. You don't have to throw away what you already know and use.

- PowerShell introduces a powerful new type of command. PowerShell commands (called *cmdlets*) share a common *Verb-Noun* syntax and offer many usability improvements over standard commands.

- PowerShell understands objects. Working directly with richly structured objects makes working with (and combining) PowerShell commands immensely easier than working in the plain-text world of traditional shells.

- PowerShell caters to administrators. Even with all its advances, PowerShell focuses strongly on its use as an interactive shell: the experience of entering commands in a running PowerShell application.

- PowerShell supports discovery. Using three simple commands, you can learn and discover almost anything PowerShell has to offer.

- PowerShell enables ubiquitous scripting. With a fully fledged scripting language that works directly from the command line, PowerShell lets you automate tasks with ease.

- PowerShell bridges many technologies. By letting you work with .NET, COM, WMI, XML, and Active Directory, PowerShell makes working with these previously isolated technologies easier than ever before.

- PowerShell simplifies management of data stores. Through its provider model, PowerShell lets you manage data stores using the same techniques you already use to manage files and folders.

We'll explore each of these pillars in this introductory tour of PowerShell. If you're running any supported version of Windows (Windows 7 or later, or Windows 2012 R2 or later), Windows PowerShell is already installed. That said, a significant step up from this default installation is the open source *PowerShell Core*.

An Interactive Shell

At its core, PowerShell is first and foremost an interactive shell. While it supports scripting and other powerful features, its focus as a shell underpins everything.

Getting started in PowerShell is a simple matter of launching *PowerShell.exe* rather than *cmd.exe*—the shells begin to diverge as you explore the intermediate and advanced functionality, but you can be productive in PowerShell immediately.

To launch PowerShell, click Start and then type **PowerShell** (or **pwsh** if you've jumped ahead!).

A PowerShell prompt window opens that's nearly identical to the traditional command prompt of its ancestors. The PS C:\Users\Lee> prompt indicates that PowerShell is ready for input, as shown in Figure P-1.

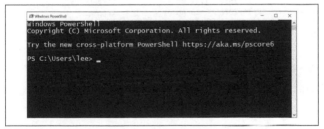

Figure P-1. Windows PowerShell, ready for input

Once you've launched your PowerShell prompt, you can enter DOS- and Unix-style commands to navigate around the filesystem just as you would with any Windows or Unix command prompt—as in the interactive session shown in Example P-1. In this example, we use the pushd, cd, dir, pwd, and popd commands to store the current location, navigate around the filesystem, list items in the current directory, and then return to the original location. Try it!

Example P-1. Entering many standard DOS- and Unix-style file manipulation commands produces the same results you get when you use them with any other Windows shell

```
PS C:\Users\Lee> function prompt { "PS > " }
PS > pushd .
PS > cd \
PS > dir

    Directory: C:\

Mode                LastWriteTime     Length Name
----                -------------     ------ ----
d----        5/8/2007   8:37 PM              Blurpark
d----        5/15/2016  4:32 PM              Chocolatey
d----        3/8/2020  12:45 PM              DXLab
d----        4/30/2020  7:00 AM              Go
d----        4/2/2016   3:05 PM              Intel
d-r--        12/15/2020 1:41 PM              Program Files
d-r--        11/28/2020 5:06 PM              Program Files (x86)
d----        5/12/2019  6:37 PM              Python27
d----        3/25/2018  1:11 PM              Strawberry
d----        12/16/2020 8:13 AM              temp
d-r--        8/11/2020  5:02 PM              Users
da---        12/16/2020 10:51 AM            Windows

PS > popd
PS > pwd

Path
----
C:\Users\Lee
```

In this example, our first command customizes the prompt. In *cmd.exe*, customizing the prompt looks like prompt PG. In Bash, it looks like PS1="[\h] \w> ". In PowerShell, you define a function that returns whatever you want displayed.

The pushd command is an alternative name (alias) to the much more descriptively named PowerShell command Push-Location. Likewise, the cd, dir, popd, and pwd commands all have more memorable counterparts.

Although navigating around the filesystem is helpful, so is running the tools you know and love, such as `ipconfig` and `notepad`. Type the command name and you'll see results like those shown in Example P-2.

Example P-2. Windows tools and applications such as ipconfig run in PowerShell just as they do in cmd.exe

```
PS > ipconfig

Windows IP Configuration

Ethernet adapter Wireless Network Connection 4:

    Connection-specific DNS Suffix .  : hsd1.wa.comcast.net.
    IP Address. . . . . . . . . . . . : 192.168.1.100
    Subnet Mask . . . . . . . . . . . : 255.255.255.0
    Default Gateway . . . . . . . . . : 192.168.1.1
PS > notepad
(notepad launches)
```

Entering `ipconfig` displays the IP addresses of your current network connections. Similarly, entering `notepad` runs—as you'd expect—the Notepad editor that ships with Windows. Try them both on your own machine.

Structured Commands (Cmdlets)

In addition to supporting traditional Windows executables, PowerShell introduces a powerful new type of command called a *cmdlet* (pronounced "command-let"). All cmdlets are named in a *Verb-Noun* pattern, such as `Get-Process`, `Get-Content`, and `Stop-Process`:

```
PS > Get-Process -Name lsass

Handles  NPM(K)  PM(K)   WS(K) VM(M)   CPU(s)   Id ProcessName
-------  ------  -----   ----- -----   ------   -- -----------
    668      13   6228    1660    46           932 lsass
```

In this example, you provide a value to the `ProcessName` parameter to get a specific process by name.

You don't always have to type these full cmdlet names, however. PowerShell lets you use the `Tab` key to autocomplete cmdlet names and parameter names:

```
PS > Get-Pro<TAB> -N<TAB> lsass
```

For quick interactive use, even that may be too much typing. To help improve your efficiency, PowerShell defines aliases for all common commands and lets you define your own. In addition to alias names, PowerShell requires only that you type enough of the parameter name to disambiguate it from the rest of the parameters in that cmdlet. PowerShell is also case-insensitive. Using the built-in `gps` alias (which represents the `Get-Process` cmdlet) along with parameter shortening, you can instead type:

```
PS > gps -n lsass
```

Going even further, PowerShell supports *positional parameters* on cmdlets. Positional parameters let you provide parameter values in a certain position on the command line, rather than having to specify them by name. The `Get-Process` cmdlet takes a process name as its first positional parameter. This parameter even supports wildcards:

```
PS > gps l*s
```

Deep Integration of Objects

PowerShell begins to flex more of its muscle as you explore the way it handles structured data and richly functional objects. For example, the following command generates a simple text

---

string. Since nothing captures that output, PowerShell displays it to you:

```
PS > "Hello World"
Hello World
```

The string you just generated is, in fact, a fully functional object from the .NET Framework. For example, you can access its Length property, which tells you how many characters are in the string. To access a property, you place a dot between the object and its property name:

```
PS > "Hello World".Length
11
```

All PowerShell commands that produce output generate that output as objects as well. For example, the Get-Process cmdlet generates a System.Diagnostics.Process object, which you can store in a variable. In PowerShell, variable names start with a $ character. If you have an instance of Notepad running, the following command stores a reference to it:

```
$process = Get-Process notepad
```

Since this is a fully functional Process object from the .NET Framework, you can call methods on that object to perform actions on it. This command calls the Kill() method, which stops a process. To access a method, you place a dot between the object and its method name:

```
$process.Kill()
```

PowerShell supports this functionality more directly through the Stop-Process cmdlet, but this example demonstrates an important point about your ability to interact with these rich objects.

Administrators as First-Class Users

While PowerShell's support for objects from the .NET Framework quickens the pulse of most users, PowerShell continues to focus strongly on administrative tasks. For example, PowerShell supports MB (for megabyte) and GB (for gigabyte) as some of its standard administrative constants. How many GIF memes will fit in a 800 GB hard drive?

```
PS > 800GB / 2.2MB
372363.636363636
```

Although the .NET Framework is traditionally a development platform, it contains a wealth of functionality useful for administrators too! In fact, it makes PowerShell a great calendar. For example, is 2096 a leap year? PowerShell can tell you:

```
PS > [DateTime]::IsLeapYear(2096)
True
```

Going further, how might you determine how much time remains until the Y2038 Epochalypse? The following command converts "01/19/2038" (the date of the Year 2038 problem) to a date, and then subtracts the current date from that. It stores the result in the $result variable, and then accesses the TotalDays property:

```
PS > $result = [DateTime] "01/19/2038" - [DateTime]::Now
PS > $result.TotalDays
6242.49822756465
```

Composable Commands

Whenever a command generates output, you can use a *pipeline character* (|) to pass that output directly to another command as input. If the second command understands the objects produced by the first command, it can operate on the results. You can chain together many commands this way, creating powerful compositions out of a few simple operations. For example, the following command gets all items in the *Path1* directory and moves them to the *Path2* directory:

```
Get-Item Path1\* | Move-Item -Destination Path2
```

You can create even more complex commands by adding additional cmdlets to the pipeline. In Example P-3, the first command gets all processes running on the system. It passes those to the Where-Object cmdlet, which runs a comparison against each incoming item. In this case, the comparison is

`$_.Handles -ge 500`, which checks whether the `Handles` property of the current object (represented by the `$_` variable) is greater than or equal to `500`. For each object in which this comparison holds true, you pass the results to the `Sort-Object` cmdlet, asking it to sort items by their `Handles` property. Finally, you pass the objects to the `Format-Table` cmdlet to generate a table that contains the `Handles`, `Name`, and `Description` of the process.

Example P-3. You can build more complex PowerShell commands by using pipelines to link cmdlets, as shown here with Get-Process, Where-Object, Sort-Object, and Format-Table

```
PS > Get-Process |
    Where-Object { $_.Handles -ge 500 } |
    Sort-Object Handles |
    Format-Table Handles,Name,Description -Auto

Handles Name     Description
------- ----     -----------
    588 winlogon
    592 svchost
    667 lsass
    725 csrss
    742 System
    964 WINWORD  Microsoft Office Word
   1112 OUTLOOK  Microsoft Office Outlook
   2063 svchost
```

Techniques to Protect You from Yourself

While aliases, wildcards, and composable pipelines are powerful, their use in commands that modify system information can easily be nerve-racking. After all, what does this command do? Think about it, but don't try it just yet:

```
PS > gps [b-t]*[c-r] | Stop-Process
```

It appears to stop all processes that begin with the letters b through t and end with the letters c through r. How can you be sure? Let PowerShell tell you. For commands that modify data,

PowerShell supports -WhatIf and -Confirm parameters that let you see what a command *would* do:

```
PS > gps [b-t]*[c-r] | Stop-Process -whatif
What if: Performing operation "Stop-Process" on "ctfmon (812)".
What if: Performing operation "Stop-Process" on "Ditto (1916)".
What if: Performing operation "Stop-Process" on "dsamain (316)".
What if: Performing operation "Stop-Process" on "ehrecvr (1832)".
What if: Performing operation "Stop-Process" on "ehSched (1852)".
What if: Performing operation "Stop-Process" on "EXCEL (2092)".
What if: Performing operation "Stop-Process" on "explorer (1900)".
(...)
```

In this interaction, using the -WhatIf parameter with the Stop-Process pipelined command lets you preview which processes on your system will be stopped before you actually carry out the operation.

Note that this example is not a dare! In the words of one reviewer:

> Not only did it stop everything, but on one of my old machines, it forced a shutdown with only one minute warning!
>
> It was very funny though…At least I had enough time to save everything first!

Common Discovery Commands

While reading through a guided tour is helpful, I find that most learning happens in an ad hoc fashion. To find all commands that match a given wildcard, use the Get-Command cmdlet. For example, by entering the following, you can find out which PowerShell commands (and Windows applications) contain the word *process*:

```
PS > Get-Command *process*
```

CommandType	Name	Definition
Cmdlet	Get-Process	Get-Process [[-Name] <Str...
Application	qprocess.exe	c:\windows\system32\qproc...
Cmdlet	Stop-Process	Stop-Process [-Id] <Int32...

To see what a command such as Get-Process does, use the Get-Help cmdlet, like this:

```
PS > Get-Help Get-Process
```

Since PowerShell lets you work with objects from the .NET Framework, it provides the Get-Member cmdlet to retrieve information about the properties and methods that an object, such as a .NET System.String, supports. Piping a string to the Get-Member command displays its type name and its members:

```
PS > "Hello World" | Get-Member

    TypeName: System.String

Name             MemberType  Definition
----             ----------  ----------
(...)
PadLeft          Method      System.String PadLeft(Int32 tota...
PadRight         Method      System.String PadRight(Int32 tot...
Remove           Method      System.String Remove(Int32 start...
Replace          Method      System.String Replace(Char oldCh...
Split            Method      System.String[] Split(Params Cha...
StartsWith       Method      System.Boolean StartsWith(String...
Substring        Method      System.String Substring(Int32 st...
ToCharArray      Method      System.Char[] ToCharArray(), Sys...
ToLower          Method      System.String ToLower(), System....
ToLowerInvariant Method      System.String ToLowerInvariant()
ToString         Method      System.String ToString(), System...
ToUpper          Method      System.String ToUpper(), System....
ToUpperInvariant Method      System.String ToUpperInvariant()
Trim             Method      System.String Trim(Params Char[]...
TrimEnd          Method      System.String TrimEnd(Params Cha...
TrimStart        Method      System.String TrimStart(Params C...
Length           Property    System.Int32 Length {get;}
```

Ubiquitous Scripting

PowerShell makes no distinction between the commands typed at the command line and the commands written in a script. Your favorite cmdlets work in scripts and your favorite scripting techniques (e.g., the foreach statement) work directly on the command line. For example, to add up the handle count for all running processes:

```
PS > $handleCount = 0
PS > foreach($process in Get-Process) {
    $handleCount += $process.Handles }
PS > $handleCount
19403
```

While PowerShell provides a command (Measure-Object) to measure statistics about collections, this short example shows how PowerShell lets you apply techniques that normally require a separate scripting or programming language.

In addition to using PowerShell scripting keywords, you can also create and work directly with objects from the .NET Framework that you may be familiar with. PowerShell becomes almost like the C# immediate mode in Visual Studio. Example P-4 shows how PowerShell lets you easily interact with the .NET Framework.

Example P-4. Using objects from the .NET Framework to retrieve a web page and process its content

```
PS > $webClient = New-Object System.Net.WebClient
PS > $content = $webClient.DownloadString(
              "https://devblogs.microsoft.com/powershell/feed/")
PS > $content.Substring(0,1000)
<?xml version="1.0" encoding="UTF-8"?><rss version="2.0"
        xmlns:content="http://purl.org/rss/1.0/modules/content/"
        xmlns:wfw="http://wellformedweb.org/CommentAPI/"
        xmlns:dc="http://purl.org/dc/elements/1.1/"
        xmlns:atom="http://www.w3.org/2005/Atom"
        xmlns:sy="http://purl.org/rss/1.0/modules/syndication/"
        xmlns:slash="http://purl.org/rss/1.0/modules/slash/" >
<channel>
        <title>PowerShell</title>
        <atom:link href="https://devblogs.microsoft.com/powersh..."
        <link>https://devblogs.microsoft.com/powershell</link>
        <description>Automating the world one-liner at a time…
        </description>
(...)
```

Ad Hoc Development

By blurring the lines between interactive administration and writing scripts, the history buffers of PowerShell sessions quickly become the basis for ad hoc script development. In this example, you call the Get-History cmdlet to retrieve the history of your session. For each item, you get its CommandLine property (the thing you typed) and send the output to a new script file.

```
PS > Get-History | ForEach-Object {
    $_.CommandLine } > c:\temp\script.ps1
PS > notepad c:\temp\script.ps1
(save the content you want to keep)
PS > c:\temp\script.ps1
```

NOTE

If this is the first time you've run a script in PowerShell, you'll need to configure your execution policy.

Bridging Technologies

We've seen how PowerShell lets you fully leverage the .NET Framework in your tasks, but its support for common technologies stretches even farther. As Example P-5 (continued from Example P-4) shows, PowerShell supports XML.

Example P-5. Working with XML content in PowerShell

```
PS > $xmlContent = [xml] $content
PS > $xmlContent

xml                         xml-stylesheet              rss
---                         --------------              ---
version="1.0" encoding...   type="text/xsl" href="...   rss

PS > $xmlContent.rss

version : 2.0
content : http://purl.org/rss/1.0/modules/content/
wfw     : http://wellformedweb.org/CommentAPI/
dc      : http://purl.org/dc/elements/1.1/
atom    : http://www.w3.org/2005/Atom
sy      : http://purl.org/rss/1.0/modules/syndication/
slash   : http://purl.org/rss/1.0/modules/slash/
channel : channel
```

```
PS > $xmlContent.rss.channel.item | select Title

title
-----
PowerShell 7.2 Preview 2 release
Announcing PowerShell Crescendo Preview.1
You've got Help!
SecretManagement preview 6 and SecretStore preview 4
Announcing PowerShell 7.1
Announcing PSReadLine 2.1+ with Predictive IntelliSense
Updating help for the PSReadLine module
PowerShell Working Groups
(...)
```

PowerShell also lets you work with Windows Management Instrumentation (WMI) and Common Information Model (CIM):

```
PS > Get-CimInstance Win32_Bios

SMBIOSBIOSVersion : ASUS A7N8X Deluxe ACPI BIOS Rev 1009
Manufacturer      : Phoenix Technologies, LTD
Name              : Phoenix - AwardBIOS v6.00PG
SerialNumber      : xxxxxxxxxxx
Version           : Nvidia - 42302e31
```

Or, as Example P-6 shows, you can work with Active Directory Service Interfaces (ADSI).

Example P-6. Working with Active Directory in PowerShell

```
PS > [ADSI] "WinNT://./Administrator" | Format-List *

UserFlags            : {66113}
MaxStorage           : {-1}
PasswordAge          : {19550795}
PasswordExpired      : {0}
LoginHours           : {255 255 255 255 255 255 255 255 255
                        255 255 255 255 255 255 255 255 255
                        255 255 255}
FullName             : {}
Description          : {Built-in account for administering
                        the computer/domain}
BadPasswordAttempts  : {0}
LastLogin            : {5/21/2007 3:00:00 AM}
HomeDirectory        : {}
```

```
LoginScript                  : {}
Profile                      : {}
HomeDirDrive                 : {}
Parameters                   : {}
PrimaryGroupID               : {513}
Name                         : {Administrator}
MinPasswordLength            : {0}
MaxPasswordAge               : {3710851}
MinPasswordAge               : {0}
PasswordHistoryLength        : {0}
AutoUnlockInterval           : {1800}
LockoutObservationInterval   : {1800}
MaxBadPasswordsAllowed       : {0}
RasPermissions               : {1}
objectSid                    : {1 5 0 0 0 0 0 5 21 0 0 0 121 227
                               252 83 122 130 50 34 67 23 10 50
                               244 1 0 0}
```

Or, as Example P-7 shows, you can even use PowerShell for scripting traditional COM objects.

Example P-7. Working with COM objects in PowerShell

```
PS > $firewall = New-Object -com HNetCfg.FwMgr
PS > $firewall.LocalPolicy.CurrentProfile


Type                                               : 1
FirewallEnabled                                    : True
ExceptionsNotAllowed                               : False
NotificationsDisabled                              : False
UnicastResponsesToMulticastBroadcastDisabled       : False
RemoteAdminSettings                                : System.__ComObject
IcmpSettings                                       : System.__ComObject
GloballyOpenPorts                                  : {Media Center
                                                     Extender Service,
                                                     Remote Media Center
                                                     Experience, Adam
                                                     Test Instance,
                                                     QWAVE...}
Services                                           : {File and Printer
                                                     Sharing, UPnP
                                                     Framework, Remote
                                                     Desktop}
AuthorizedApplications                             : {Remote Assistance,
                                                     Windows Messenger,
                                                     Media Center,
                                                     Trillian...}
```

Namespace Navigation Through Providers

Another avenue PowerShell offers for working with the system is *providers*. PowerShell providers let you navigate and manage data stores using the same techniques you already use to work with the filesystem, as illustrated in Example P-8.

Example P-8. Navigating the filesystem

```
PS > Set-Location c:\
PS > Get-ChildItem


    Directory: C:\


Mode                LastWriteTime         Length Name
----                -------------         ------ ----
d----         5/8/2007   8:37 PM                Blurpark
d----         5/15/2016  4:32 PM                Chocolatey
d----         3/8/2020  12:45 PM                DXLab
d----         4/30/2020  7:00 AM                Go
d----         4/2/2016   3:05 PM                Intel
d-r--        12/15/2020  1:41 PM                Program Files
d-r--        11/28/2020  5:06 PM                Program Files (x86)
d----         5/12/2019  6:37 PM                Python27
d----         3/25/2018  1:11 PM                Strawberry
d----        12/16/2020  8:13 AM                temp
d-r--         8/11/2020  5:02 PM                Users
da---        12/16/2020 10:51 AM                Windows
```

This also works on the registry, as shown in Example P-9.

Example P-9. Navigating the registry

```
PS > Set-Location HKCU:\Software\Microsoft\Windows\
PS > Get-ChildItem


    Hive: HKEY_CURRENT_USER\Software\Microsoft\Windows


Name                    Property
----                    --------
CurrentVersion
DWM                     Composition         : 1
                        ColorPrevalence     : 0
                        ColorizationColor   : 3290322719
                        EnableAeroPeek      : 1
```

```
                  AccentColor                : 4280243998
                  EnableWindowColorization   : 1
Shell
TabletPC
Windows Error Reporting

PS > Set-Location CurrentVersion\Run
PS > Get-ItemProperty .

(...)
OneDrive       : "C:\Users\lee\AppData\Local\Microsoft\OneDriv..."
    /background
OpenDNS Updater : "C:\Program Files (x86)\OpenDNS Updater\OpenD..."
    /autostart
Ditto          : C:\Program Files\Ditto\Ditto.exe
(...)
```

And it even works on the machine's certificate store, as
Example P-10 illustrates.

Example P-10. Navigating the certificate store

```
PS > Set-Location cert:\CurrentUser\Root
PS > Get-ChildItem

    Directory: Microsoft.PowerShell.Security\
        Certificate::CurrentUser\Root

Thumbprint                          Subject
----------                          -------
CDD4EEAE6000AC7F40C3802C171E30148   CN=Microsoft Root Certificate...
BE36A4562FB2EE05DBB3D32323ADF4450   CN=Thawte Timestamping CA, OU...
A43489159A520F0D93D032CCAF37E7FE2   CN=Microsoft Root Authority, ...
9FE47B4D05D46E8066BAB1D1BFC9E48F1   CN=PowerShell Local Certifica...
7F88CD7223F3C813818C994614A89C99F   CN=Microsoft Authenticode(tm)...
245C97DF7514E7CF2DF8BE72AE957B9E0   OU=Copyright (c) 1997 Microso...
(...)
```

Much, Much More

As exciting as this guided tour was, it barely scratches the sur-
face of how you can use PowerShell to improve your productivity and systems management skills.

Conventions Used in This Book

The following typographical conventions are used in this book:

Italic
> Indicates new terms, URLs, email addresses, filenames, and file extensions.

`Constant width`
> Used for program listings, as well as within paragraphs to refer to program elements such as variable or function names, databases, data types, environment variables, statements, and keywords.

`Constant width bold`
> Shows commands or other text that should be typed literally by the user.

`Constant width italic`
> Shows text that should be replaced with user-supplied values or by values determined by context.

Using Code Examples

Supplemental material (code examples, exercises, etc.) is available for download at *https://github.com/LeeHolmes/PowerShell Cookbook*.

If you have a technical question or a problem using the code examples, please send an email to *bookquestions@oreilly.com*.

This book is here to help you get your job done. In general, if example code is offered with this book, you may use it in your programs and documentation. You do not need to contact us for permission unless you're reproducing a significant portion of the code. For example, writing a program that uses several chunks of code from this book does not require permission. Selling or distributing examples from O'Reilly books does require permission. Answering a question by citing this book and quoting example code does not require permission. Incorporating a significant amount of example code from this book into your product's documentation does require permission.

We appreciate, but generally do not require, attribution. An attribution usually includes the title, author, publisher, and ISBN. For example: "*PowerShell Pocket Reference* by Lee Holmes (O'Reilly), 3rd edition. Copyright 2021 Lee Holmes, 978-1-098-10167-1."

If you feel your use of code examples falls outside fair use or the permission given above, feel free to contact us at *permissions@oreilly.com*.

O'Reilly Online Learning

For more than 40 years, *O'Reilly Media* has provided technology and business training, knowledge, and insight to help companies succeed.

Our unique network of experts and innovators share their knowledge and expertise through books, articles, and our online learning platform. O'Reilly's online learning platform gives you on-demand access to live training courses, in-depth learning paths, interactive coding environments, and a vast collection of text and video from O'Reilly and 200+ other publishers. For more information, visit *http://oreilly.com*.

How to Contact Us

Please address comments and questions concerning this book to the publisher:

O'Reilly Media, Inc.
1005 Gravenstein Highway North
Sebastopol, CA 95472
800-998-9938 (in the United States or Canada)
707-829-0515 (international or local)
707-829-0104 (fax)

We have a web page for this book, where we list errata, examples, and any additional information. You can access this page at *https://oreil.ly/powershell-pocket-3rd*.

Email *bookquestions@oreilly.com* to comment or ask technical questions about this book.

For news and information about our books and courses, visit *http://oreilly.com*.

Find us on Facebook: *http://facebook.com/oreilly*

Follow us on Twitter: *http://twitter.com/oreillymedia*

Watch us on YouTube: *http://youtube.com/oreillymedia*

## CHAPTER 1

PowerShell Language and Environment

Commands and Expressions

PowerShell breaks any line that you enter into its individual units (*tokens*), and then interprets each token in one of two ways: as a command or as an expression. The difference is subtle: expressions support logic and flow control statements (such as if, foreach, and throw), whereas commands do not.

You will often want to control the way that PowerShell interprets your statements, so Table 1-1 lists the available options.

Table 1-1. PowerShell evaluation controls

Statement	Explanation
Precedence control: ( )	Forces the evaluation of a command or expression, similar to the way that parentheses are used to force the order of evaluation in a mathematical expression. For example: PS > 5 * (1 + 2) 15 PS > (dir).Count 227

Statement	Explanation
Expression subparse: $()	Forces the evaluation of a command or expression, similar to the way that parentheses are used to force the order of evaluation in a mathematical expression.
	However, a subparse is as powerful as a subprogram and is required only when the subprogram contains logic or flow control statements.
	This statement is also used to expand dynamic information inside a string.
	For example:

```
PS > "The answer is (2+2)"
The answer is (2+2)

PS > "The answer is $(2+2)"
The answer is 4

PS > $value = 10
PS > $result = $(
    if($value -gt 0) { $true }
    else { $false })
PS > $result
True
```

Statement	Explanation
List evaluation: @()	Forces an expression to be evaluated as a list. If it is already a list, it will remain a list. If it is not, PowerShell temporarily treats it as one.
	For example:

```
PS > "Hello".Length
5
PS > @("Hello").Length
1
PS > ([PSCustomObject] @{
Property1 = "Hello"
Count = 100 }).Count
100
PS > @([PSCustomObject] @{
Property1 = "Hello"
Count = 100 }).Count
1
```

Statement	Explanation

DATA evaluation: DATA { }	Evaluates the given script block in the context of the PowerShell data language. The data language supports only data-centric features of the PowerShell language.
	
	For example:
	`PS > DATA { 1 + 1 }`
	`2`
	`PS > DATA { $myVariable = "Test" }`
	`Assignment statements are not`
	`allowed in restricted language`
	`mode or a Data section.`

Comments

To create single-line comments, begin a line with the # character. To create a block (or multiline) comment, surround the region with the characters <# and #>:

```
# This is a regular comment

<# This is a block comment

function MyTest
{
    "This should not be considered a function"
}

$myVariable = 10;

Block comment ends
#>

# This is regular script again
```

Help Comments

PowerShell creates help for your script or function by looking at its comments. If the comments include any supported help tags, PowerShell adds those to the help for your command.

Comment-based help supports the following tags, which are all case-insensitive:

.SYNOPSIS

A short summary of the command, ideally a single sentence.

.DESCRIPTION

A more detailed description of the command.

.PARAMETER *name*

A description of parameter *name*, with one for each parameter you want to describe. While you can write a .PARAMETER comment for each parameter, PowerShell also supports comments written directly above the parameter. Putting parameter help alongside the actual parameter makes it easier to read and maintain.

.EXAMPLE

An example of this command in use, with one for each example you want to provide. PowerShell treats the line immediately beneath the .EXAMPLE tag as the example command. If this line doesn't contain any text that looks like a prompt, PowerShell adds a prompt before it. It treats lines that follow the initial line as additional output and example commentary.

.INPUTS

A short summary of pipeline input(s) supported by this command. For each input type, PowerShell's built-in help follows this convention:

```
System.String
    You can pipe a string that contains a path to
    Get-ChildItem.
```

.OUTPUTS

A short summary of items generated by this command. For each output type, PowerShell's built-in help follows this convention:

```
System.ServiceProcess.ServiceController
    This cmdlet returns objects that represent the
    services on the computer.
```

.NOTES

Any additional notes or remarks about this command.

.LINK

A link to a related help topic or command, with one .LINK
tag per link. If the related help topic is a URL, PowerShell
launches that URL when the user supplies the -Online
parameter to Get-Help for your command.

While these are all of the supported help tags you are likely to
use, comment-based help also supports tags for some of
Get-Help's more obscure features:

- .COMPONENT
- .ROLE
- .FUNCTIONALITY
- .FORWARDHELPTARGETNAME
- .FORWARDHELPCATEGORY
- .REMOTEHELPRUNSPACE
- .EXTERNALHELP

For more information about these tags, type **Get-Help
about_Comment_Based_Help**.

Variables

PowerShell provides several ways to define and access variables,
as summarized in Table 1-2.

Table 1-2. PowerShell variable syntaxes

Syntax	Meaning
`$simpleVariable = "Value"`	A simple variable name. The variable name must consist of alphanumeric characters. Variable names are not case-sensitive.
`$variable1, $variable2 = "Value1", "Value2"`	Multiple variable assignment. PowerShell populates each variable from the value in the corresponding position on the righthand side. Extra values are assigned as a list to the last variable listed.
`${ arbitrary!@#@ \#{var}iable } = "Value"`	An arbitrary variable name. The variable name must be surrounded by curly braces, but it may contain any characters. Curly braces in the variable name must be escaped with a backtick (`` ` ``).
`${c:\filename. extension}`	Variable "Get and Set Content" syntax. This is similar to the arbitrary variable name syntax. If the name corresponds to a valid PowerShell path, you can get and set the content of the item at that location by reading and writing to the variable.
`[datatype] $variable = "Value"`	Strongly typed variable. Ensures that the variable may contain only data of the type you declare. PowerShell throws an error if it cannot coerce the data to this type when you assign it.
`[constraint] $variable = "Value"`	Constrained variable. Ensures that the variable may contain only data that passes the supplied validation constraints: `[ValidateLength(4, 10)] $a = "Hello"` The supported validation constraints are the same as those supported as parameter validation attributes.

Syntax	Meaning
`$SCOPE:variable`	Gets or sets the variable at that specific scope. Valid scope names are `global` (to make a variable available to the entire shell), `script` (to make a variable available only to the current script or persistent during module commands), `local` (to make a variable available only to the current scope and subscopes), and `private` (to make a variable available only to the current scope). The default scope is the *current* scope: `global` when defined interactively in the shell, `script` when defined outside any functions or script blocks in a script, and `local` elsewhere.
`New-Item Variable:` `\variable -Value value`	Creates a new variable using the variable provider.
`Get-Item Variable:` `\variable` `Get-Variable variable`	Gets the variable using the variable provider or `Get-Variable` cmdlet. This lets you access extra information about the variable, such as its options and description.
`New-Variable variable` `-Option option -Value value`	Creates a variable using the `New-Variable` cmdlet. This lets you provide extra information about the variable, such as its options and description.

NOTE

Unlike some languages, PowerShell rounds (rather than truncates) numbers when it converts them to the [int] data type:

```
PS > (3/2)
1.5
PS > [int] (3/2)
2
```

Booleans

Boolean (true or false) variables are most commonly initialized to their literal values of $true and $false. When PowerShell evaluates variables as part of a Boolean expression (for example, an if statement), though, it maps them to a suitable Boolean representation, as listed in Table 1-3.

Table 1-3. PowerShell Boolean interpretations

Result	Boolean representation
$true	True
$false	False
$null	False
Nonzero number	True
Zero	False
Nonempty string	True
Empty string	False
Empty array	False
Single-element array	The Boolean representation of its single element
Multi-element array	True
Hashtable (either empty or not)	True

Strings

PowerShell offers several facilities for working with plain-text data.

Literal and Expanding Strings

To define a literal string (one in which no variable or escape expansion occurs), enclose it in single quotes:

```
$myString = 'hello `t $ENV:SystemRoot'
```

$myString gets the actual value of hello `t $ENV:SystemRoot.

To define an expanding string (one in which variable and escape expansion occur), enclose it in double quotes:

```
$myString = "hello `t $ENV:SystemRoot"
```

$myString gets a value similar to hello C:\WINDOWS.

To include a single quote in a single-quoted string or a double quote in a double-quoted string, include two of the quote characters in a row:

```
PS > "Hello ""There""!"
Hello "There"!
PS > 'Hello ''There''!'
Hello 'There'!
```

NOTE

To include a complex expression inside an expanding string, use a subexpression. For example:

```
$prompt = "$(Get-Location) >"
```

$prompt gets a value similar to c:\temp >.

Accessing the properties of an object requires a subexpression:

```
$version = "Current PowerShell version is:"
    $PSVersionTable.PSVersion.Major
```

$version gets a value similar to:

```
Current PowerShell version is: 3
```

Here Strings

To define a *here string* (one that may span multiple lines), place the two characters @" at the beginning and the two characters "@ on their own line at the end.

For example:

```
$myHereString = @"
This text may span multiple lines, and may
contain "quotes."
"@
```

Here strings may be of either the literal (single-quoted) or expanding (double-quoted) variety.

Escape Sequences

PowerShell supports escape sequences inside strings, as listed in Table 1-4.

Table 1-4. PowerShell escape sequences

Sequence	Meaning
`` `0 ``	The *null* character. Often used as a record separator.
`` `a ``	The *alarm* character. Generates a beep when displayed on the console.
`` `b ``	The *backspace* character. The previous character remains in the string but is overwritten when displayed on the console.
`` `e ``	The *escape* character. Marks the beginning of an ANSI escape sequence such as "`` `e[2J ``".
`` `f ``	A *form feed*. Creates a page break when printed on most printers.
`` `n ``	A *newline*.
`` `r ``	A *carriage return*. Newlines in PowerShell are indicated entirely by the `` `n `` character, so this is rarely required.
`` `t ``	A *tab*.
`` `u{hex-code} ``	A *unicode character literal*. Creates a character represented by the specified hexadecimal Unicode code point, such as `` `u{2265} `` (≥).

Sequence	Meaning
`` `v ``	A *vertical tab*.
`' '` (two single quotes)	A *single quote*, when in a literal string.
`" "` (two double quotes)	A *double quote*, when in an expanding string.
`` `any other character ``	That character, taken literally.

Numbers

PowerShell offers several options for interacting with numbers and numeric data.

Simple Assignment

To define a variable that holds numeric data, simply assign it as you would other variables. PowerShell automatically stores your data in a format that is sufficient to accurately hold it:

```
$myInt = 10

$myUnsignedInt = 10u
$myUnsignedInt = [uint] 10
```

$myInt gets the value of 10, as a (32-bit) integer. $myUnsignedInt gets the value of 10 as an unsigned integer.

```
$myDouble = 3.14
```

$myDouble gets the value of 3.14, as a (53-bit, 9 bits of precision) double.

To explicitly assign a number as a byte (8-bit) or short (16-bit) number, use the y or s suffixes. Prefixing either with u creates an unsigned version of that data type. You can also use the [byte], [int16], and [short] casts:

```
$myByte = 127y
$myByte = [byte] 127
$myUnsignedByte = 127uy

$myShort = 32767s
$myShort = [int16] 32767
$myShort = [short] 32767
```

```
$myUnsignedShort = 32767us
$myUnsignedShort = [ushort] 32767
```

To explicitly assign a number as a long (64-bit) integer or decimal (96-bit, 96 bits of precision), use the long (l) and decimal (d) suffixes. You can also use the [long] cast:

```
$myLong = 2147483648l
$myLong = [long] 2147483648

$myUnsignedLong = 2147483648ul
$myUnsignedLong = [ulong] 2147483648

$myDecimal = 0.999d
```

To explicitly assign a number as a BigInteger (an arbitrary large integer with no upper or lower bounds), use the BigInteger (n) suffix:

```
$myBigInt = 99999999999999999999999999999999n
```

PowerShell also supports scientific notation, where e<*number*> represents multiplying the original number by the <*number*> power of 10:

```
$myPi = 3141592653e-9
```

$myPi gets the value of 3.141592653.

The data types in PowerShell (integer, long integer, double, and decimal) are built on the .NET data types of the same names.

Administrative Numeric Constants

Since computer administrators rarely get the chance to work with numbers in even powers of 10, PowerShell offers the numeric constants of pb, tb, gb, mb, and kb to represent petabytes (1,125,899,906,842,624), terabytes (1,099,511,627,776), gigabytes (1,073,741,824), megabytes (1,048,576), and kilobytes (1,024), respectively:

```
PS > $downloadTime = (1gb + 250mb) / 120kb
PS > $downloadTime
10871.4666666667
```

You can combine these numeric multipliers with a data type as long as the result fits in that data type, such as 250ngb.

Hexadecimal and Other Number Bases

To directly enter a hexadecimal number, use the hexadecimal prefix 0x:

```
$myErrorCode = 0xFE4A
```

$myErrorCode gets the integer value 65098.

To directly enter a binary number, use the binary prefix 0b:

```
$myBinary = 0b101101010101
```

$myBinary gets the integer value of 2901.

If you don't know the hex or binary value as a constant or need to convert into Octal, use the [Convert] class from the .NET Framework. The first parameter is the value to convert, and the second parameter is the base (2, 8, 10, or 16):

```
$myOctal = [Convert]::ToInt32("1234567", 8)
```

$myOctal gets the integer value of 342391.

```
$myHexString = [Convert]::ToString(65098, 16)
```

$myHexString gets the string value of fe4a.

```
$myBinaryString = [Convert]::ToString(12345, 2)
```

$myBinaryString gets the string value of 11000000111001.

NOTE

See "Working with the .NET Framework" on page 49 to learn more about using PowerShell to interact with the .NET Framework.

Large Numbers

To work with extremely large numbers, use the BigInt class.

```
[BigInt]::Pow(12345, 123)
```

To do math with several large numbers, use the [BigInt] cast (or the n BigInt data type) for all operands:

```
PS > 98123498123498123894n * 98123498123498123894n
9628220883992139841085109029337773723236

PS > $val = "98123498123498123894"
PS > ([BigInt] $val) * ([BigInt] $val)
9628220883992139841085109029337773723236
```

Imaginary and Complex Numbers

To work with imaginary and complex numbers, use the System.Numerics.Complex class:

```
PS > [System.Numerics.Complex]::ImaginaryOne *
    [System.Numerics.Complex]::ImaginaryOne | Format-List

Real      : -1
Imaginary : 0
Magnitude : 1
Phase     : 3.14159265358979
```

Arrays and Lists

Array Definitions

PowerShell arrays hold lists of data. The @() (*array cast*) syntax tells PowerShell to treat the contents between the parentheses as an array. To create an empty array, type:

```
$myArray = @()
```

To define a nonempty array, use a comma to separate its elements:

```
$mySimpleArray = 1,"Two",3.14
```

Arrays may optionally be only a single element long:

```
$myList = ,"Hello"
```

Or, alternatively (using the array cast syntax):

```
$myList = @("Hello")
```

Elements of an array don't need to be all of the same data type, unless you declare it as a strongly typed array. In the following example, the outer square brackets define a strongly typed variable (as mentioned in "Variables" on page 5), and int[] represents an array of integers:

```
[int[]] $myArray = 1,2,3.14
```

In this mode, PowerShell generates an error if it cannot convert any of the elements in your list to the required data type. In this case, it rounds 3.14 to the integer value of 3:

```
PS > $myArray[2]
3
```

NOTE

To ensure that PowerShell treats collections of uncertain length (such as history lists or directory listings) as a list, use the list evaluation syntax @(...) described in "Commands and Expressions" on page 1.

Arrays can also be multidimensional *jagged* arrays (arrays within arrays):

```
$multiDimensional = @(
    (1,2,3,4),
    (5,6,7,8)
  )
```

$multiDimensional[0][1] returns 2, coming from row 0, column 1.

$multiDimensional[1][3] returns 8, coming from row 1, column 3.

To define a multidimensional array that is not jagged, create a multidimensional instance of the .NET type. For integers, that would be an array of System.Int32:

```
$multidimensional = New-Object "Int32[,]" 2,4
$multidimensional[0,1] = 2
$multidimensional[1,3] = 8
```

Array Access

To access a specific element in an array, use the [] operator. PowerShell numbers your array elements starting at zero. Using $myArray = 1,2,3,4,5,6 as an example:

```
$myArray[0]
```

returns 1, the first element in the array.

```
$myArray[2]
```

returns 3, the third element in the array.

```
$myArray[-1]
```

returns 6, the last element of the array.

```
$myArray[-2]
```

returns 5, the second-to-last element of the array.

You can also access ranges of elements in your array:

```
PS > $myArray[0..2]
1
2
3
```

returns elements 0 through 2, inclusive.

```
PS > $myArray[-1..2]
6
1
2
3
```

returns the final element, wraps around, and returns elements 0 through 2, inclusive. PowerShell wraps around because the first number in the range is negative, and the second number in the range is positive.

```
PS > $myArray[-1..-3]
6
5
4
```

returns the last element of the array through to the third-to-last element in the array, in descending order. PowerShell does not wrap around (and therefore scans backward in this case) because both numbers in the range share the same sign.

If the array being accessed might be *null*, you can use the null conditional array access operator (?[]). The result of the expression will be *null* if the array being accessed did not exist. It will be the element at the specified index otherwise:

```
(Get-Process -id 0).Modules?[0]
```

Array Slicing

You can combine several of the statements in the previous section at once to extract more complex ranges from an array. Use the + sign to separate array ranges from explicit indexes:

```
$myArray[0,2,4]
```

returns the elements at indices 0, 2, and 4.

```
$myArray[0,2+4..5]
```

returns the elements at indices 0, 2, and 4 through 5, inclusive.

```
$myArray[,0+2..3+0,0]
```

returns the elements at indices 0, 2 through 3 inclusive, 0, and 0 again.

NOTE

You can use the array slicing syntax to create arrays as well:

```
$myArray = ,0+2..3+0,0
```

Hashtables (Associative Arrays)

Hashtable Definitions

PowerShell *hashtables* (also called *associative arrays*) let you
associate keys with values. To define a hashtable, use the syntax:

```
$myHashtable = @{}
```

You can initialize a hashtable with its key/value pairs when you
create it. PowerShell assumes that the keys are strings, but the
values may be any data type:

```
$myHashtable = @{ Key1 = "Value1"; "Key 2" = 1,2,3; 3.14 = "Pi" }
```

To define a hashtable that retains its insertion order, use the
[ordered] cast:

```
$orderedHash = [ordered] @{}
$orderedHash["NewKey"] = "Value"
```

Hashtable Access

To access or modify a specific element in an associative array,
you can use either the array-access or property-access syntax:

```
$myHashtable["Key1"]
```

returns "Value1".

```
$myHashtable."Key 2"
```

returns the array 1,2,3.

```
$myHashtable["New Item"] = 5
```

adds "New Item" to the hashtable.

```
$myHashtable."New Item" = 5
```

also adds "New Item" to the hashtable.

XML

PowerShell supports XML as a native data type. To create an
XML variable, cast a string to the [xml] type:

```
$myXml = [xml] @"
<AddressBook>
   <Person contactType="Personal">
      <Name>Lee</Name>
      <Phone type="home">555-1212</Phone>
      <Phone type="work">555-1213</Phone>
   </Person>
   <Person contactType="Business">
      <Name>Ariel</Name>
      <Phone>555-1234</Phone>
   </Person>
</AddressBook>
"@
```

PowerShell exposes all child nodes and attributes as properties. When it does this, PowerShell automatically groups children that share the same node type:

`$myXml.AddressBook`

returns an object that contains a Person property.

`$myXml.AddressBook.Person`

returns a list of Person nodes. Each person node exposes contactType, Name, and Phone as properties.

`$myXml.AddressBook.Person[0]`

returns the first Person node.

`$myXml.AddressBook.Person[0].ContactType`

returns Personal as the contact type of the first Person node.

Simple Operators

Once you have defined your data, the next step is to work with it.

Arithmetic Operators

The arithmetic operators let you perform mathematical operations on your data, as shown in Table 1-5.

The System.Math class in the .NET Framework offers many powerful operations in addition to the native operators supported by PowerShell:

```
PS > [Math]::Pow([Math]::E, [Math]::Pi)
23.1406926327793
```

See "Working with the .NET Framework" on page 49 to learn more about using PowerShell to interact with the .NET Framework.

Table 1-5. PowerShell arithmetic operators

Operator	Meaning
+	The *addition operator:* `$leftValue + $rightValue` When used with numbers, returns their sum. When used with strings, returns a new string created by appending the second string to the first. When used with arrays, returns a new array created by appending the second array to the first. When used with hashtables, returns a new hashtable created by merging the two hashtables. Since hashtable keys must be unique, PowerShell returns an error if the second hashtable includes any keys already defined in the first hashtable. When used with any other type, PowerShell uses that type's addition operator (`op_Addition`) if it implements one.
–	The *subtraction operator:* `$leftValue - $rightValue` When used with numbers, returns their difference. This operator does not apply to strings, arrays, or hashtables. When used with any other type, PowerShell uses that type's subtraction operator (`op_Subtraction`) if it implements one.

Operator	Meaning
*	The *multiplication operator*: `$leftValue * $rightValue` When used with numbers, returns their product. When used with strings (`"=" * 80`), returns a new string created by appending the string to itself the number of times you specify. When used with arrays (`1..3 * 7`), returns a new array created by appending the array to itself the number of times you specify. This operator does not apply to hashtables. When used with any other type, PowerShell uses that type's multiplication operator (`op_Multiply`) if it implements one.
/	The *division operator*: `$leftValue / $rightValue` When used with numbers, returns their quotient. This operator does not apply to strings, arrays, or hashtables. When used with any other type, PowerShell uses that type's division operator (`op_Division`) if it implements one.
%	The *modulus operator*: `$leftValue % $rightValue` When used with numbers, returns the remainder of their division. This operator does not apply to strings, arrays, or hashtables. When used with any other type, PowerShell uses that type's modulus operator (`op_Modulus`) if it implements one.

+=
-=
*=
/=
%=
	Assignment operators:
	`$variable operator= value`
	
	These operators match the simple arithmetic operators (+, −, *, /, and %) but store the result in the variable on the lefthand side of the operator. It is a short form for
	`$variable = $variable operator value.`

Logical Operators

The logical operators let you compare Boolean values, as shown in Table 1-6.

Table 1-6. PowerShell logical operators

Operator	Meaning

-and	*Logical AND*:
	`$leftValue -and $rightValue`
	
	Returns `$true` if both lefthand and righthand arguments evaluate to `$true`. Returns `$false` otherwise.
	You can combine several `-and` operators in the same expression:
	`$value1 -and $value2 -and $value3 ...`
	
	PowerShell implements the `-and` operator as a short-circuit operator and evaluates arguments only if all arguments preceding it evaluate to `$true`.

-or	*Logical OR*:
	`$leftValue -or $rightValue`
	
	Returns `$true` if the lefthand or righthand arguments evaluate to `$true`. Returns `$false` otherwise.
	You can combine several `-or` operators in the same expression:
	`$value1 -or $value2 -or $value3 ...`
	
	PowerShell implements the `-or` operator as a short-circuit operator and evaluates arguments only if all arguments preceding it evaluate to `$false`.

-xor	*Logical exclusive OR*: `$leftValue -xor $rightValue` Returns `$true` if either the lefthand or righthand argument evaluates to `$true`, but not if both do. Returns `$false` otherwise.
-not !	*Logical NOT*: `-not $value` Returns `$true` if its righthand (and only) argument evaluates to `$false`. Returns `$false` otherwise.

Binary Operators

The binary operators, listed in Table 1-7, let you apply the Boolean logical operators bit by bit to the operator's arguments. When comparing bits, a 1 represents $true, whereas a 0 represents $false.

Table 1-7. PowerShell binary operators

Operator	Meaning

-band	*Binary AND*:
	`$leftValue -band $rightValue`
	
	Returns a number where bits are set to 1 if the bits of the lefthand and righthand arguments at that position are both 1. All other bits are set to 0. For example:
	`PS > $int1 = 0b110110110`
	`PS > $int2 = 0b010010010`
	`PS > $result = $int1 -band $int2`
	`PS > [Convert]::ToString($result, 2)`
	`10010010`

-bor	*Binary OR*:
	`$leftValue -bor $rightValue`
	
	Returns a number where bits are set to 1 if either of the bits of the lefthand and righthand arguments at that position is 1. All other bits are set to 0. For example:
	`PS > $int1 = 0b110110110`
	`PS > $int2 = 0b010010010`
	`PS > $result = $int1 -bor $int2`
	`PS > [Convert]::ToString($result, 2)`
	`110110110`

Operator	Meaning

-bxor   *Binary exclusive OR*:
         $leftValue -bxor *$rightValue*

Returns a number where bits are set to 1 if either of the bits of the lefthand and righthand arguments at that position is 1, but not if both are. All other bits are set to 0. For example:

```
PS > $int1 = 0b110110110
PS > $int2 = 0b010010010
PS > $result = $int1 -bxor $int2
PS > [Convert]::ToString($result, 2)
100100100
```

-bnot   *Binary NOT*:
         -bnot *$value*

Returns a number where bits are set to 1 if the bit of the righthand (and only) argument at that position is set to 1. All other bits are set to 0. For example:

```
PS > $int1 = 0b110110110
PS > $result = -bnot $int1
PS > [Convert]::ToString($result, 2)
11111111111111111111111001001001
```

-shl   *Binary shift left*:
         $value -slh *$count*

Shifts the bits of a number to the left *$count* places. Bits on the righthand side are set to 0. For example:

```
PS > $int1 = 438
PS > [Convert]::ToString($int1, 2)
110110110

PS > $result = $int1 -shl 5
PS > [Convert]::ToString($result, 2)
11011011000000
```

Operator	Meaning

-shr   *Binary shift right:*
        $value -slr *$count*

Shifts the bits of a number to the right *$count* places. For signed
values, bits on the lefthand side have their sign preserved. For
example:

```
PS > $int1 = -2345
PS > [Convert]::ToString($int1, 2)
11111111111111111111011011010111

PS > $result = $int1 -shr 3
PS > [Convert]::ToString($result, 2)
11111111111111111111111011011010
```

Other Operators

PowerShell supports several other simple operators, as listed
here.

-replace (Replace operator)

The *replace operator* returns a new string, where the text in
"target" that matches the regular expression *"pattern"* has
been replaced with the replacement text *"replacement"*:

"target" -replace *"pattern"*,*"replacement"*

The following returns a new string, where the text in *"target"*
that matches the regular expression *"pattern"* has been
replaced with the output value of the script block supplied. In
the script block, the $_ variable represents the current
System.Text.RegularExpressions.Match:

"target" -replace *"pattern"*,{ *scriptblock* }

By default, PowerShell performs a case-insensitive comparison.
The -ireplace operator makes this case-insensitivity explicit,
whereas the -creplace operator performs a case-sensitive
comparison.

If the regular expression pattern contains named captures or capture groups, the replacement string may reference those as well. For example:

```
PS > "Hello World" -replace "(.*) (.*)",'$2 $1'
World Hello
```

If *"target"* represents an array, the -replace operator operates on each element of that array.

For more information on the details of regular expressions, see Chapter 2.

-f (Format operator)

The *format operator* returns a string where the format items in the format string have been replaced with the text equivalent of the values in the value array:

```
"Format String" -f values
```

For example:

```
PS > "{0:n0}" -f 1000000000
1,000,000,000
```

The format string for the format operator is exactly the format string supported by the .NET String.Format method.

For more details about the syntax of the format string, see Chapter 4.

-as (Type conversion operator)

The *type conversion operator* returns $value cast to the given .NET type:

```
$value -as [Type]
```

If this conversion is not possible, PowerShell returns $null. For example:

```
PS > 3/2 -as [int]
2
PS > $result = "Hello" -as [int]
PS > $result -eq $null
True
```

-split (Split operator)

The *unary split operator* breaks the given input string into an array, using whitespace (\s+) to identify the boundary between elements:

```
-split "Input String"
```

It also trims the results. For example:

```
PS > -split "  Hello     World    "
Hello
World
```

The *binary split operator* breaks the given input string into an array, using the given *delimiter* or *script block* to identify the boundary between elements:

```
"Input String" -split "delimiter",maximum,options
"Input String" -split { Scriptblock },maximum
```

Delimiter is interpreted as a regular expression match. *Script block* is called for each character in the input, and a split is introduced when it returns $true.

Maximum defines the maximum number of elements to be returned, leaving unsplit elements as the last item. This item is optional. Use "0" for unlimited if you want to provide options but not alter the maximum.

Options define special behavior to apply to the splitting behavior. The possible enumeration values are:

SimpleMatch
> Split on literal strings, rather than regular expressions they may represent.

RegexMatch
> Split on regular expressions. This option is the default.

CultureInvariant
> Does not use culture-specific capitalization rules when doing a case-insensitive split.

IgnorePatternWhitespace

> Ignores spaces and regular expression comments in the split pattern.

Multiline

> Allows the ^ and $ characters to match line boundaries, not just the beginning and end of the content.

Singleline

> Treats the ^ and $ characters as the beginning and end of the content. This option is the default.

IgnoreCase

> Ignores the capitalization of the content when searching for matches.

ExplicitCapture

> In a regular expression match, only captures named groups. This option has no impact on the -split operator.

For example:

```
PS > "1a2B3" -split "[a-z]+",0,"IgnoreCase"
1
2
3
```

-join (Join operator)

The *unary join operator* combines the supplied items into a single string, using no separator:

```
-join ("item1","item2",...,"item_n")
```

For example:

```
PS > -join ("a","b")
ab
```

The *binary join operator* combines the supplied items into a single string, using *Delimiter* as the separator:

```
("item1","item2",...,"item_n") -join Delimiter
```

For example:

```
PS > ("a","b") -join ", "
a, b
```

Comparison Operators

The PowerShell comparison operators, listed in Table 1-8, let you compare expressions against each other. By default, PowerShell's comparison operators are case-insensitive. For all operators where case sensitivity applies, the -i prefix makes this case insensitivity explicit, whereas the -c prefix performs a case-sensitive comparison.

Table 1-8. PowerShell comparison operators

Operator	Meaning
-eq	The *equality operator*: *$leftValue* -eq *$rightValue* For all primitive types, returns $true if *$leftValue* and *$rightValue* are equal. When used with arrays, returns all elements in *$leftValue* that are equal to *$rightValue*. When used with any other type, PowerShell uses that type's Equals() method if it implements one.
-ne	The *negated equality operator*: *$leftValue* -ne *$rightValue* For all primitive types, returns $true if *$leftValue* and *$rightValue* are not equal. When used with arrays, returns all elements in *$leftValue* that are not equal to *$rightValue*. When used with any other type, PowerShell returns the negation of that type's Equals() method if it implements one.

Operator	Meaning
-ge	The *greater-than-or-equal operator*: *$leftValue* -ge *$rightValue* For all primitive types, returns $true if *$leftValue* is greater than or equal to *$rightValue*. When used with arrays, returns all elements in *$leftValue* that are greater than or equal to *$rightValue*. When used with any other type, PowerShell returns the result of that object's Compare() method if it implements one. If the method returns a number greater than or equal to zero, the operator returns $true.
-gt	The *greater-than operator*: $leftValue -gt $rightValue For all primitive types, returns $true if *$leftValue* is greater than *$rightValue*. When used with arrays, returns all elements in *$leftValue* that are greater than *$rightValue*. When used with any other type, PowerShell returns the result of that object's Compare() method if it implements one. If the method returns a number greater than zero, the operator returns $true.
-in	The *in operator*: *$value* -in *$list* Returns $true if the value *$value* is contained in the list *$list*. That is, if $item -eq $value returns $true for at least one item in the list. This is equivalent to the -contains operator with the operands reversed.
-notin	The *negated in operator*: Returns $true when the -in operator would return $false.

Operator	Meaning
-lt	The *less-than operator*: $leftValue -lt $rightValue For all primitive types, returns $true if $leftValue is less than $rightValue. When used with arrays, returns all elements in $leftValue that are less than $rightValue. When used with any other type, PowerShell returns the result of that object's Compare() method if it implements one. If the method returns a number less than zero, the operator returns $true.
-le	The *less-than-or-equal operator*: $leftValue -le $rightValue For all primitive types, returns $true if $leftValue is less than or equal to $rightValue. When used with arrays, returns all elements in $leftValue that are less than or equal to $rightValue. When used with any other type, PowerShell returns the result of that object's Compare() method if it implements one. If the method returns a number less than or equal to zero, the operator returns $true.

Operator	Meaning

-like	The *like operator*:
	`$leftValue -like Pattern`
	
	Evaluates the pattern against the target, returning `$true` if the simple match is successful.
	When used with arrays, returns all elements in `$leftValue` that match `Pattern`.
	The -like operator supports the following simple wildcard characters:
	
	• ?: Any single unspecified character
	
	• *: Zero or more unspecified characters
	
	• [a-b]: Any character in the range of a–b
	
	• [ab]: The specified characters a or b
	
	For example:
	`PS > "Test" -like "[A-Z]e?[tr]"`
	`True`

-notlike	The *negated like operator*: Returns `$true` when the -like operator would return `$false`.

Operator	Meaning

-match	The *match operator*:
	`"Target" -match Regular Expression`
	
	Evaluates the regular expression against the target, returning $true if the match is successful. Once complete, PowerShell places the successful matches in the $matches variable.
	When used with arrays, returns all elements in *Target* that match *Regular Expression*.
	The $matches variable is a hashtable that maps the individual matches to the text they match. 0 is the entire text of the match, 1 and on contain the text from any unnamed captures in the regular expression, and string values contain the text from any named captures in the regular expression.
	For example:
	`PS > "Hello World" -match "(.*) (.*)"`
	`True`
	`PS > $matches[1]`
	`Hello`
	
	For more information on the details of regular expressions, see Chapter 2.

-notmatch	The *negated match operator*: Returns $true when the -match operator would return $false. The -notmatch operator still populates the $matches variable with the results of match.
-contains	The *contains operator*: `$list -contains $value` Returns $true if the list specified by $list contains the value $value—that is, if $item -eq $value returns $true for at least one item in the list. This is equivalent to the -in operator with the operands reversed.

Operator	Meaning
-notcontains	The *negated contains operator:* Returns $true when the -contains operator would return $false.
-is	The *type operator:* *$leftValue* -is *[type]* Returns $true if *$value* is (or extends) the specified .NET type.
-isnot	The *negated type operator:* Returns $true when the -is operator would return $false.

Conditional Statements

Conditional statements in PowerShell let you change the flow of execution in your script.

if, elseif, and else Statements

```
if(condition)
{
    statement block
}
elseif(condition)
{
    statement block
}
else
{
    statement block
}
```

If *condition* evaluates to $true, PowerShell executes the statement block you provide. Then, it resumes execution at the end of the if/elseif/else statement list. PowerShell requires the enclosing braces around the statement block, even if the statement block contains only one statement.

If *condition* evaluates to $false, PowerShell evaluates any following (optional) elseif conditions until one matches. If one matches, PowerShell executes the statement block associated with that condition, and then resumes execution at the end of the if/elseif/else statement list.

For example:

```
$textToMatch = Read-Host "Enter some text"
$matchType = Read-Host "Apply Simple or Regex matching?"
$pattern = Read-Host "Match pattern"
if($matchType -eq "Simple")
{
    $textToMatch -like $pattern
}
elseif($matchType -eq "Regex")
{
    $textToMatch -match $pattern
}
else
{
    Write-Host "Match type must be Simple or Regex"
}
```

If none of the conditions evaluate to $true, PowerShell executes the statement block associated with the (optional) else clause, and then resumes execution at the end of the if/elseif/else statement list.

To apply an if statement to each element of a list and filter it to return only the results that match the supplied condition, use the Where-Object cmdlet or .where() method:

```
Get-Process | Where-Object { $_.Handles -gt 500 }

(Get-Process).where( { $_.Handles -gt 500} )
```

Ternary Operators

```
$result = condition ? true value : false value
```

A short-form version of an if/else statement. If *condition* evaluates to $true, the result of the expression is the value of the *true value* clause. Otherwise, the result of the expression is the value of the *false value* clause. For example:

```
(Get-Random) % 2 -eq 0 ? "Even number" : "Odd number"
```

Null Coalescing and Assignment Operators

```
$result = nullable value ?? default value
```

Assignment version:

```
$result = nullable value
$result ??= default value
```

A short-form version of a ternary operator that only checks if the expression is *null* or not. If it is null, the result of the expression is the value of the *default value* clause. For example:

```
Get-Process | ForEach-Object { $_.CPU ?? "<Unavailable>" }
```

or

```
$cpu = (Get-Process -id 0).CPU
$cpu ??= "Unavailable"
```

switch Statements

```
switch options expression
{
   comparison value            { statement block }
   -or-
   { comparison expression }   { statement block }
   (...)
   default                     { statement block }
}
```

or:

```
switch options -file filename
{
   comparison value            { statement block }
   -or
   { comparison expression }   { statement block }
```

```
    (...)
    default                   { statement block }
}
```

When PowerShell evaluates a switch statement, it evaluates
expression against the statements in the switch body. If
expression is a list of values, PowerShell evaluates each item
against the statements in the switch body. If you specify the
-file option, PowerShell treats the lines in the file as though
they were a list of items in *expression*.

The *comparison value* statements let you match the current
input item against the pattern specified by *comparison value*.
By default, PowerShell treats this as a case-insensitive exact
match, but the options you provide to the switch statement can
change this, as shown in Table 1-9.

Table 1-9. Options supported by PowerShell switch statements

Option	Meaning
-casesensitive -c	*Case-sensitive match.* With this option active, PowerShell executes the associated statement block only if the current input item exactly matches the value specified by *comparison value*. If the current input object is a string, the match is case-sensitive.
-exact -e	*Exact match* With this option active, PowerShell executes the associated statement block only if the current input item exactly matches the value specified by *comparison value*. This match is case-insensitive. This is the default mode of operation.
-regex -r	*Regular-expression match* With this option active, PowerShell executes the associated statement block only if the current input item matches the regular expression specified by *comparison value*. This match is case-insensitive.

Option	Meaning
-wildcard	*Wildcard match*
-w	With this option active, PowerShell executes the associated statement block only if the current input item matches the wildcard specified by *comparison value.*
	The wildcard match supports the following simple wildcard characters:

- ?: Any single unspecified character
- *: Zero or more unspecified characters
- [a-b]: Any character in the range of a–b
- [ab]: The specified characters a or b

This match is case-insensitive.

The { *comparison expression* } statements let you process the current input item, which is stored in the $_ (or $PSItem) variable, in an arbitrary script block. When it processes a { *comparison expression* } statement, PowerShell executes the associated statement block only if { *comparison expression* } evaluates to $true.

PowerShell executes the statement block associated with the (optional) default statement if no other statements in the switch body match.

When processing a switch statement, PowerShell tries to match the current input object against each statement in the switch body, falling through to the next statement even after one or more have already matched. To have PowerShell discontinue the current comparison (but retry the switch statement with the next input object), include a continue statement as the last statement in the statement block. To have PowerShell exit a switch statement completely after it processes a match, include a break statement as the last statement in the statement block.

For example:

```
$myPhones = "(555) 555-1212","555-1234"

switch -regex ($myPhones)
{
  { $_.Length -le 8 }  { "Area code was not specified"; break }
  { $_.Length -gt 8 }  { "Area code was specified" }
  "\((555)\).*"        { "In the $($matches[1]) area code" }
}
```

produces the output:

```
Area code was specified
In the 555 area code
Area code was not specified
```

NOTE

See the next section on Looping Statements for more information about the break statement.

By default, PowerShell treats this as a case-insensitive exact match, but the options you provide to the switch statement can change this.

Looping Statements

Looping statements in PowerShell let you execute groups of statements multiple times.

for Statement

```
:loop_label for (initialization; condition; increment)
{
    statement block
}
```

When PowerShell executes a for statement, it first executes the expression given by *initialization*. It next evaluates *condition*. If *condition* evaluates to $true, PowerShell executes the given statement block. It then executes the expression given by *increment*. PowerShell continues to execute the statement block and *increment* statement as long as *condition* evaluates to $true.

For example:

```
for($counter = 0; $counter -lt 10; $counter++)
{
    Write-Host "Processing item $counter"
}
```

The break and continue statements (discussed in "Flow Control Statements" on page 42) can specify the *loop_label* of any enclosing looping statement as their target.

foreach Statement

```
:loop_label foreach(variable in expression)
{
    statement block
}
```

When PowerShell executes a foreach statement, it executes the pipeline given by *expression*—for example, Get-Process | Where-Object {$_.Handles -gt 500} or 1..10. For each item produced by the expression, it assigns that item to the variable specified by *variable* and then executes the given statement block. For example:

```
$handleSum = 0
foreach($process in Get-Process |
    Where-Object { $_.Handles -gt 500 })
{
    $handleSum += $process.Handles
}
$handleSum
```

In addition to the foreach statement, you can also use the foreach method on collections directly:

```
$handleSum = 0
(Get-Process).foreach( { $handleSum += $_.Handles } )
```

The break and continue statements (discussed in "Flow Control Statements" on page 42) can specify the *loop_label* of any enclosing looping statement as their target. In addition to the foreach statement, PowerShell also offers the ForEach-Object cmdlet with similar capabilities.

while Statement

```
:loop_label while(condition)
{
    statement block
}
```

When PowerShell executes a while statement, it first evaluates the expression given by *condition*. If this expression evaluates to $true, PowerShell executes the given statement block. PowerShell continues to execute the statement block as long as *condition* evaluates to $true. For example:

```
$command = "";
while($command -notmatch "quit")
{
    $command = Read-Host "Enter your command"
}
```

The break and continue statements (discussed in "Flow Control Statements" on page 42) can specify the *loop_label* of any enclosing looping statement as their target.

do ... while Statement/do ... until Statement

```
:loop_label do
{
    statement block
} while(condition)
```

or

```
:loop_label do
{
    statement block
} until(condition)
```

When PowerShell executes a do ... while or do ... until statement, it first executes the given statement block. In a do ... while statement, PowerShell continues to execute the statement block as long as *condition* evaluates to $true. In a do ... until statement, PowerShell continues to execute the statement as long as *condition* evaluates to $false. For example:

```
$validResponses = "Yes","No"
$response = ""
do
{
    $response = Read-Host "Yes or No?"
} while($validResponses -notcontains $response)
"Got $response"

$response = ""
do
{
    $response = Read-Host "Yes or No?"
} until($validResponses -contains $response)
"Got $response"
```

The break and continue statements (discussed in the next section) can specify the *loop_label* of any enclosing looping statement as their target.

Flow Control Statements

PowerShell supports two statements to help you control flow within loops: break and continue.

break

The break statement halts execution of the current loop. PowerShell then resumes execution at the end of the current looping statement, as though the looping statement had completed naturally. For example:

```
for($counter = 0; $counter -lt 5; $counter++)
{
    for($counter2 = 0; $counter2 -lt 5; $counter2++)
    {
        if($counter2 -eq 2)
        {
            break
        }

        Write-Host "Processing item $counter,$counter2"
    }
}
```

produces the output (notice the second column never reaches the value 2):

```
Processing item 0,0
Processing item 0,1
Processing item 1,0
Processing item 1,1
Processing item 2,0
Processing item 2,1
Processing item 3,0
Processing item 3,1
Processing item 4,0
Processing item 4,1
```

If you specify a label with the break statement—for example, break outer_loop—PowerShell halts the execution of that loop instead. For example:

```
:outer_loop for($counter = 0; $counter -lt 5; $counter++)
{
    for($counter2 = 0; $counter2 -lt 5; $counter2++)
    {
        if($counter2 -eq 2)
        {
            break outer_loop
        }

        Write-Host "Processing item $counter,$counter2"
    }
}
```

produces the output:

```
Processing item 0,0
Processing item 0,1
```

continue

The continue statement skips execution of the rest of the current statement block. PowerShell then continues with the next iteration of the current looping statement, as though the statement block had completed naturally. For example:

```
for($counter = 0; $counter -lt 5; $counter++)
{
    for($counter2 = 0; $counter2 -lt 5; $counter2++)
    {
        if($counter2 -eq 2)
```

```
        {
            continue
        }

        Write-Host "Processing item $counter,$counter2"
    }
}
```

produces the output:

```
Processing item 0,0
Processing item 0,1
Processing item 0,3
Processing item 0,4
Processing item 1,0
Processing item 1,1
Processing item 1,3
Processing item 1,4
Processing item 2,0
Processing item 2,1
Processing item 2,3
Processing item 2,4
Processing item 3,0
Processing item 3,1
Processing item 3,3
Processing item 3,4
Processing item 4,0
Processing item 4,1
Processing item 4,3
Processing item 4,4
```

If you specify a label with the continue statement—for example, continue outer_loop—PowerShell continues with the next iteration of that loop instead.

For example:

```
:outer_loop for($counter = 0; $counter -lt 5; $counter++)
{
    for($counter2 = 0; $counter2 -lt 5; $counter2++)
    {
        if($counter2 -eq 2)
        {
            continue outer_loop
        }

        Write-Host "Processing item $counter,$counter2"
    }
}
```

produces the output:

```
Processing item 0,0
Processing item 0,1
Processing item 1,0
Processing item 1,1
Processing item 2,0
Processing item 2,1
Processing item 3,0
Processing item 3,1
Processing item 4,0
Processing item 4,1
```

Classes

```
## A class called "Example" that inherits from "BaseClass"
## and implements the "ImplementedInterface" interface
class Example : BaseClass, ImplementedInterface
{
    ## Default constructor, which also invokes the constructor
    ## from the base class.
    Example() : base()
    {
        [Example]::lastInstantiated = Get-Date
    }

    ## Constructor with parameters
    Example([string] $Name)
    {
        $this.Name = $Name
        [Example]::lastInstantiated = Get-Date
    }

    ## A publicly visible property with validation attributes
    [ValidateLength(2,20)]
    [string] $Name

    ## A property that is hidden from default views
    static hidden [DateTime] $lastInstantiated

    ## A publicly visible method that returns a value
    [string] ToString()
    {
        ## Return statement is required. Implicit / pipeline output
        ## is not treated as output like it is with functions.
        return $this.ToString( [Int32]::MaxValue )
    }

    ## A publicly visible method that returns a value
```

```
[string] ToString([int] $MaxLength)
{
    $output = "Name = $($this.Name);"
        "LastInstantiated = $([Example]::lastInstantiated)"
    $outputLength = [Math]::Min($MaxLength, $output.Length)
    return $output.Substring(0, $outputLength)
}

}
```

Base classes and interfaces

To define a class that inherits from a base class or implements an interfaces, provide the base class and/or interface names after the class name, separated by a colon (deriving from a base class or implementing any interfaces is optional):

```
class Example [: BaseClass, ImplementedInterface]
```

Constructors

To define a class constructor, create a method with the same name as the class. You can define several constructors, including those with parameters. To automatically call a constructor from the base class, add : base() to the end of the method name:

```
Example() [: base()]
```

```
Example([int] $Parameter1, [string] $Parameter2) [: base()]
```

Properties

To define a publicly visible property, define a PowerShell variable in your class. As with regular Powershell variables, you may optionally add validation attributes or declare a type constraint for the property:

```
[ValidateLength(2,20)]
[string] $Name
```

To hide the property from default views (similar to a member variable in other languages), use the hidden keyword. Users are still able to access hidden properties if desired: they are just removed from default views. You can make a property static if you want it to be shared with all instances of your class in the current process:

```
static hidden [DateTime] $lastInstantiated
```

Methods

Define a method as though you would define a PowerShell function, but without the *function* keyword and without the param() statement. Methods support parameters, parameter validation, and can also have the same name as long as their parameters differ:

```
[string] ToString() { ... }

[string] ToString([int] $MaxLength) { ... }
```

Custom Enumerations

To define a custom enumeration, use the enum keyword:

```
enum MyColor {
  Red = 1
  Green = 2
  Blue = 3
}
```

If enumeration values are intended to be combined through bitwise operators, use the [Flags()] attribute. If you require that the enumerated values derive from a specific integral data type (byte, sbyte, short, ushort, int, uint, long or ulong), provide that data type after the colon character:

```
[Flags()] enum MyColor : uint {
  Red = 1
  Green = 2
  Blue = 4
}
```

Workflow-Specific Statements

Within a workflow, PowerShell supports three statements not supported in traditional PowerShell scripts: InlineScript, Parallel, and Sequence.

InlineScript

The InlineScript keyword defines an island of PowerShell
script that will be invoked as a unit, and with traditional
PowerShell scripting semantics. For example:

```
workflow MyWorkflow
{
    ## Method invocation not supported in a workflow
    ## [Math]::Sqrt(100)

    InlineScript
    {
        ## Supported in an InlineScript
        [Math]::Sqrt(100)
    }
}
```

Parallel/Sequence

The Parallel keyword specifies that all statements within the
statement block should run in parallel. To group statements
that should be run as a unit, use the Sequence keyword:

```
workflow MyWorkflow
{
    Parallel
    {
        InlineScript { Start-Sleep -Seconds 2;
            "One thing run in parallel" }
        InlineScript { Start-Sleep -Seconds 4;
            "Another thing run in parallel" }
        InlineScript { Start-Sleep -Seconds 3;
            "A third thing run in parallel" }

        Sequence
        {
            Start-Sleep -Seconds 1
            "A fourth"
```

```
            "and fifth thing run as a unit, in parallel"
        }
    }
}
```

Note that you should not use PowerShell Workflows for the parallel statement alone—the `-Parallel` parameter to the `ForEach-Object` cmdlet is much more efficient.

Working with the .NET Framework

One feature that gives PowerShell its incredible reach into both system administration and application development is its capability to leverage Microsoft's enormous and broad .NET Framework.

Working with the .NET Framework in PowerShell comes mainly by way of one of two tasks: calling methods or accessing properties.

Static Methods

To call a static method on a class, type:

```
[ClassName]::MethodName(parameter list)
```

For example:

```
PS > [System.Diagnostics.Process]::GetProcessById(0)
```

gets the process with the ID of 0 and displays the following output:

```
Handles  NPM(K)    PM(K)    WS(K) VM(M)  CPU(s)    Id ProcessName
-------  ------    -----    ----- -----  ------    -- -----------
      0       0        0       16     0             0 Idle
```

Instance Methods

To call a method on an instance of an object, type:

```
$objectReference.MethodName(parameter list)
```

For example:

```
PS > $process = [System.Diagnostics.Process]::GetProcessById(0)
PS > $process.Refresh()
```

This stores the process with ID of 0 into the $process variable. It then calls the Refresh() instance method on that specific process.

Explicitly Implemented Interface Methods

To call a method on an explictly implemented interface, type:

```
([Interface] $objectReference).MethodName(parameter list)
```

For example:

```
PS > ([IConvertible] 123).ToUint16($null)
```

Static Properties

To access a static property on a class, type:

```
[ClassName]::PropertyName
```

or:

```
[ClassName]::PropertyName = value
```

For example, the [System.DateTime] class provides a Now static property that returns the current time:

```
PS > [System.DateTime]::Now
Sunday, July 16, 2006 2:07:20 PM
```

Although this is rare, some types let you set the value of some static properties.

Instance Properties

To access an instance property on an object, type:

```
$objectReference.PropertyName
```

or:

```
$objectReference.PropertyName = value
```

For example:

```
PS > $today = [System.DateTime]::Now
PS > $today.DayOfWeek
Sunday
```

This stores the current date in the $today variable. It then calls the DayOfWeek instance property on that specific date.

If the value of the property might be *null*, you can use the null conditional property access operator (?.). The result of the expression will be *null* if any property in the chain did not exist. It will be the final property's value otherwise:

```
(Get-Process -Id 0)?.MainModule?.Filename
```

Learning About Types

The two primary avenues for learning about classes and types are the Get-Member cmdlet and the documentation for the .NET Framework.

The Get-Member cmdlet

To learn what methods and properties a given type supports, pass it through the Get-Member cmdlet, as shown in Table 1-10.

Table 1-10. Working with the Get-Member cmdlet

Action	Result
[typename] | Get-Member -Static	All the static methods and properties of a given type.
$objectReference | Get-Member -Static	All the static methods and properties provided by the type in *$objectReference*.

Action	Result
$objectReference | Get-Member	All the instance methods and properties provided by the type in $objectReference. If $objectReference represents a collection of items, PowerShell returns the instances and properties of the types contained by that collection. To view the instances and properties of a collection itself, use the -InputObject parameter of Get-Member: Get-Member -InputObject $objectReference
[typename] | Get-Member	All the instance methods and properties of a System.RuntimeType object that represents this type.

.NET Framework documentation

Another source of information about the classes in the .NET Framework is the documentation itself, available through the search facilities at Microsoft's developer documentation site (*https://docs.microsoft.com*).

Typical documentation for a class first starts with a general overview, and then provides a hyperlink to the members of the class—the list of methods and properties it supports.

NOTE

To get to the documentation for the members quickly, search for them more explicitly by adding the term "members" to your search term:

classname members

The documentation for the members of a class lists their constructors, methods, properties, and more. It uses an S icon to represent the static methods and properties. Click the member name for more information about that member, including the type of object that the member produces.

Type Shortcuts

When you specify a type name, PowerShell lets you use a short form for some of the most common types, as listed in Table 1-11.

Table 1-11. PowerShell type shortcuts

Type shortcut	Full classname
[Adsi]	[System.DirectoryServices.DirectoryEntry]
[AdsiSearcher]	[System.DirectoryServices.DirectorySearcher]
[Float]	[System.Single]
[Hashtable]	[System.Collections.Hashtable]
[Int]	[System.Int32]
[IPAddress]	[System.Net.IPAddress]
[Long]	[System.Collections.Int64]
[PowerShell]	[System.Management.Automation.PowerShell]
[PSCustomObject]	[System.Management.Automation.PSObject]
[PSModuleInfo]	[System.Management.Automation.PSModuleInfo]
[PSObject]	[System.Management.Automation.PSObject]
[Ref]	[System.Management.Automation.PSReference]
[Regex]	[System.Text.RegularExpressions.Regex]

Type shortcut	Full classname
[Runspace]	[System.Management.Automation.Runspaces.Runspace]
[RunspaceFactory]	[System.Management.Automation.Runspaces.RunspaceFactory]
[ScriptBlock]	[System.Management.Automation.ScriptBlock]
[Switch]	[System.Management.Automation.SwitchParameter]
[Wmi]	[System.Management.ManagementObject]
[WmiClass]	[System.Management.ManagementClass]
[WmiSearcher]	[System.Management.ManagementObjectSearcher]
[Xml]	[System.Xml.XmlDocument]
[*TypeName*]	[System.*TypeName*]

Creating Instances of Types

```
$objectReference = New-Object TypeName parameters
$objectReference = [TypeName]::new(parameters)
```

Although static methods and properties of a class generate objects, you'll often want to create them explicitly yourself. PowerShell's New-Object cmdlet lets you create an instance of the type you specify. The parameter list must match the list of parameters accepted by one of the type's constructors, as described in the SDK documentation.

For example:

```
$webClient = New-Object Net.WebClient
$webClient.DownloadString("http://search.msn.com")
```

If the type represents a generic type, enclose its type parameters in square brackets:

```
PS > $hashtable =
    New-Object "System.Collections.Generic.Dictionary[String,Bool]"
PS > $hashtable["Test"] = $true
```

Most common types are available by default. However, many types are available only after you load the library (called the *assembly*) that defines them. The Microsoft documentation for a class includes the assembly that defines it.

To load an assembly, use the -AssemblyName parameter of the Add-Type cmdlet:

```
PS > Add-Type -AssemblyName System.Web
PS > [System.Web.HttpUtility]::UrlEncode("http://www.bing.com")
http%3a%2f%2fwww.bing.com
```

To update the list of namespaces that PowerShell searches by default, specify that namespace in a using statement:

```
PS > using namespace System.Web
PS > [HttpUtility]::UrlEncode("http://www.bing.com")
```

Interacting with COM Objects

PowerShell lets you access methods and properties on COM objects the same way you would interact with objects from the .NET Framework. To interact with a COM object, use its ProgId with the -ComObject parameter (often shortened to -Com) on New-Object:

```
PS > $shell = New-Object -Com Shell.Application
PS > $shell.Windows() | Select-Object LocationName,LocationUrl
```

For more information about the COM objects most useful to system administrators, see Chapter 8.

Extending Types

PowerShell supports two ways to add your own methods and properties to any type: the Add-Member cmdlet and a custom types extension file.

The Add-Member cmdlet

The `Add-Member` cmdlet lets you dynamically add methods, properties, and more to an object. It supports the extensions shown in Table 1-12.

Table 1-12. Selected member types supported by the Add-Member cmdlet

Member type	Meaning
AliasProperty	A property defined to alias another property:
| | ```
PS > $testObject = [PsObject] "Test"
PS > $testObject |
    Add-Member "AliasProperty" Count Length
PS > $testObject.Count
4
``` |
CodeProperty	A property defined by a `System.Reflection. MethodInfo`.
	This method must be public, static, return results (nonvoid), and take one parameter of type `PsObject`.
NoteProperty	A property defined by the initial value you provide:
| | ```
PS > $testObject = [PsObject] "Test"
PS > $testObject |
    Add-Member NoteProperty Reversed tseT
PS > $testObject.Reversed
tseT
``` |
| ScriptProperty | A property defined by the script block you provide. In that script block, `$this` refers to the current instance: |
| | ```
PS > $testObject = [PsObject] ("Hi" * 100)
PS > $testObject |
    Add-Member ScriptProperty IsLong {
        $this.Length -gt 100
    }
PS > $testObject.IsLong

True
``` |
```

Member type	Meaning
PropertySet	A property defined as a shortcut to a set of properties. Used in cmdlets such as Select-Object: ```\nPS > $testObject = [PsObject] [DateTime]::Now\nPS > $collection = New-Object `\n Collections.ObjectModel.Collection[String]\n$collection.Add("Month")\n$collection.Add("Year")\n$testObject |\n Add-Member PropertySet MonthYear $collection\n$testObject	select MonthYear\n``` ```\nMonth Year\n----- ----\n 3 2010\n```
CodeMethod	A method defined by a System.Reflection. MethodInfo. This method must be public, static, and take one parameter of type PsObject.
ScriptMethod	A method defined by the script block you provide. In that script block, $this refers to the current instance, and $args refers to the input parameters: ```\nPS > $testObject = [PsObject] "Hello"\nPS > $testObject |\n Add-Member ScriptMethod IsLong {\n $this.Length -gt $args[0]\n }\nPS > $testObject.IsLong(3)\nTrue\n\nPS > $testObject.IsLong(100)\nFalse\n```

Custom type extension files

While the Add-Member cmdlet lets you customize individual objects, PowerShell also supports configuration files that let you customize all objects of a given type. For example, you might want to add a Reverse() method to all strings or a

HelpUrl property (based on the documentation URLs) to all types.

PowerShell adds several type extensions to the file *types.ps1xml*, in the PowerShell installation directory. This file is useful as a source of examples, but you should not modify it directly. Instead, create a new one and use the Update-TypeData cmdlet to load your customizations. The following command loads *Types.custom.ps1xml* from the same directory as your profile:

```
$typesFile = Join-Path (Split-Path $profile) "Types.Custom.Ps1Xml"
Update-TypeData -PrependPath $typesFile
```

Writing Scripts, Reusing Functionality

When you want to start packaging and reusing your commands, the best place to put them is in scripts, functions, and script blocks. A *script* is a text file that contains a sequence of PowerShell commands. A *function* is also a sequence of PowerShell commands, but is usually placed within a script to break it into smaller, more easily understood segments. A script block is a function with no name. All three support the same functionality, except for how you define them.

Writing Commands

Writing scripts

To write a script, write your PowerShell commands in a text editor and save the file with a *.ps1* extension.

Writing functions

Functions let you package blocks of closely related commands into a single unit that you can access by name:

```
function SCOPE:name(parameters)
{
    statement block
}
```

or:

```
filter SCOPE:name(parameters)
{
    statement block
}
```

Valid scope names are global (to create a function available to the entire shell), script (to create a function available only to the current script), local (to create a function available only to the current scope and subscopes), and private (to create a function available only to the current scope). The default scope is the local scope, which follows the same rules as those of default variable scopes.

The content of a function's statement block follows the same rules as the content of a script. Functions support the $args array, formal parameters, the $input enumerator, cmdlet keywords, pipeline output, and equivalent return semantics.

NOTE

A common mistake is to call a function as you would call a method:

```
$result = GetMyResults($item1, $item2)
```

PowerShell treats functions as it treats scripts and other commands, so this should instead be:

```
$result = GetMyResults $item1 $item2
```

The first command passes an array that contains the items $item1 and $item2 to the GetMyResults function.

A filter is simply a function where the statements are treated as though they are contained within a process statement block. For more information about process statement blocks, see "Cmdlet keywords in commands" on page 71.

Commands in your script can access only functions that have already been defined. This can often make large scripts difficult to understand when the beginning of the script is composed entirely of helper functions. Structuring a script in the following manner often makes it more clear:

```
function Main
{
    (...)
    HelperFunction
    (...)
}

function HelperFunction
{
    (...)
}

. Main
```

Writing script blocks

```
$objectReference =
{
    statement block
}
```

PowerShell supports script blocks, which act exactly like unnamed functions and scripts. Like both scripts and functions, the content of a script block's statement block follows the same rules as the content of a function or script. Script blocks support the $args array, formal parameters, the $input enumerator, cmdlet keywords, pipeline output, and equivalent return semantics.

As with both scripts and functions, you can either invoke or dot-source a script block. Since a script block does not have a name, you either invoke it directly (& { "Hello"}) or invoke the variable (& $objectReference) that contains it.

Running Commands

There are two ways to execute a command (script, function, or script block): by invoking it or by dot-sourcing it.

Invoking

Invoking a command runs the commands inside it. Unless explicitly defined with the GLOBAL scope keyword, variables and functions defined in the script do not persist once the script exits.

NOTE

By default, a security feature in PowerShell called the Execution Policy prevents scripts from running. When you want to enable scripting in PowerShell, you must change this setting. To understand the different execution policies available to you, type `Get-Help about_signing`. After selecting an execution policy, use the `Set-Execution Policy` cmdlet to configure it:

```
Set-ExecutionPolicy RemoteSigned
```

If the command name has no spaces, simply type its name:

```
c:\temp\Invoke-Commands.ps1 parameter1 parameter2 ...
Invoke-MyFunction parameter1 parameter2 ...
```

To run the command as a background job, use the background operator (&):

```
c:\temp\Invoke-Commands.ps1 parameter1 parameter2 ... &
```

You can use either a fully qualified path or a path relative to the current location. If the script is in the current directory, you must explicitly say so:

```
.\Invoke-Commands.ps1 parameter1 parameter2 ...
```

If the command's name has a space (or the command has no name, in the case of a script block), you invoke the command by using the invoke/call operator (&) with the command name as the parameter:

```
& "C:\My Scripts\Invoke-Commands.ps1" parameter1 parameter2 ...
```

Script blocks have no name, so you place the variable holding them after the invocation operator:

```
$scriptBlock = { "Hello World" }
& $scriptBlock parameter1 parameter2 ...
```

If you want to invoke the command within the context of a module, provide a reference to that module as part of the invocation:

```
$module = Get-Module PowerShellCookbook
& $module Invoke-MyFunction parameter1 parameter2 ...
& $module $scriptBlock parameter1 parameter2 ...
```

Dot-sourcing

Dot-sourcing a command runs the commands inside it. Unlike simply invoking a command, variables and functions defined in the script *do* persist after the script exits.

You invoke a script by using the dot operator (.) and providing the command name as the parameter:

```
. "C:\Script Directory\Invoke-Commands.ps1" Parameters
. Invoke-MyFunction parameters
. $scriptBlock parameters
```

When dot-sourcing a script, you can use either a fully qualified path or a path relative to the current location. If the script is in the current directory, you must explicitly say so:

```
. .\Invoke-Commands.ps1 Parameters
```

If you want to dot-source the command within the context of a module, provide a reference to that module as part of the invocation:

```
$module = Get-Module PowerShellCookbook
. $module Invoke-MyFunction parameters
. $module $scriptBlock parameters
```

Parameters

Commands that require or support user input do so through parameters. You can use the Get-Command cmdlet to see the parameters supported by a command:

```
PS > Get-Command Stop-Process -Syntax

Stop-Process [-Id] <int[]> [-PassThru] [-Force] [-WhatIf] [...]
Stop-Process -Name <string[]> [-PassThru] [-Force] [-WhatIf] [...]
Stop-Process [-InputObject] <Process[]> [-PassThru] [-Force] [...]
```

In this case, the supported parameters of the Stop-Process command are Id, Name, InputObject, PassThru, Force, WhatIf, and Confirm.

To supply a value for a parameter, use a dash character, followed by the parameter name, followed by a space, and then the parameter value:

```
Stop-Process -Id 1234
```

If the parameter value contains spaces, surround it with quotes:

```
Stop-Process -Name "Process With Spaces"
```

If a variable contains a value that you want to use for a parameter, supply that through PowerShell's regular variable reference syntax:

```
$name = "Process With Spaces"
Stop-Process -Name $name
```

If you want to use other PowerShell language elements as a parameter value, surround the value with parentheses:

```
Get-Process -Name ("Power" + "Shell")
```

You only need to supply enough of the parameter name to disambiguate it from the rest of the parameters:

```
Stop-Process -N "Process With Spaces"
```

If a command's syntax shows the parameter name in square brackets (such as [-Id]), then it is *positional* and you may omit the parameter name and supply only the value. PowerShell supplies these unnamed values to parameters in the order of their position:

```
Stop-Process 1234
```

Rather than explicitly providing parameter names and values, you can provide a hashtable that defines them and use the *splatting operator*:

```
$parameters = @{
    Path = "c:\temp"
    Recurse = $true
}

Get-ChildItem @parameters
```

To define the default value to be used for the parameter of a command (if the parameter value is not specified directly), assign a value to the PSDefaultParameterValues hashtable. The keys of this hashtable are command names and parameter names, separated by a colon. Either (or both) may use wildcards. The values of this hashtable are either simple parameter values, or script blocks that will be evaluated dynamically:

```
PS > $PSDefaultParameterValues["Get-Process:ID"] = $pid
PS > Get-Process

PS > $PSDefaultParameterValues["Get-Service:Name"] = {
    Get-Service -Name * | ForEach-Object Name | Get-Random }
PS > Get-Service
```

Providing Input to Commands

PowerShell offers several options for processing input to a command.

Argument array

To access the command-line arguments by position, use the argument array that PowerShell places in the $args special variable:

```
$firstArgument = $args[0]
$secondArgument = $args[1]
$argumentCount = $args.Count
```

Formal parameters

To define a command with simple parameter support:

```
param(
    [TypeName] $VariableName = Default,
    ...
)
```

To define one with support for advanced functionality:

```
[CmdletBinding(cmdlet behavior customizations)]
param(
    [Parameter(Mandatory = $true, Position = 1, ...)]
    [Alias("MyParameterAlias")]
    [...]
    [TypeName] $VariableName = Default,
    ...
)
```

Formal parameters let you benefit from some of the many benefits of PowerShell's consistent command-line parsing engine.

PowerShell exposes your parameter names (for example, $VariableName) the same way that it exposes parameters in cmdlets. Users need to type only enough of your parameter name to disambiguate it from the rest of the parameters.

If you define a command with simple parameter support, PowerShell attempts to assign the input to your parameters by their position if the user does not type parameter names.

When you add the [CmdletBinding()] attribute, [Parameter()] attribute, or any of the validation attributes, PowerShell adds support for advanced parameter validation.

Command behavior customizations

The elements of the [CmdletBinding()] attribute describe how your script or function interacts with the system:

SupportsShouldProcess = $true
> If $true, enables the -WhatIf and -Confirm parameters, which tells the user that your command modifies the system and can be run in one of these experimental modes. When specified, you must also call the

`$psCmdlet.ShouldProcess()` method before modifying system state. When not specified, the default is `$false`.

`DefaultParameterSetName = `*`name`*

Defines the default parameter set name of this command. This is used to resolve ambiguities when parameters declare multiple sets of parameters and the user input doesn't supply enough information to pick between available parameter sets. When not specified, the command has no default parameter set name.

`ConfirmImpact = `*`"High"`*

Defines this command as one that should have its confirmation messages (generated by the `$psCmdlet.ShouldProcess()` method) shown by default. More specifically, PowerShell defines three confirmation impacts: `Low`, `Medium`, and `High`. PowerShell generates the cmdlet's confirmation messages automatically whenever the cmdlet's impact level is greater than the preference variable. When not specified, the command's impact is `Medium`.

Parameter attribute customizations

The elements of the `[Parameter()]` attribute mainly define how your parameter behaves in relation to other parameters (all elements are optional):

`Mandatory = $true`

Defines the parameter as mandatory. If the user doesn't supply a value to this parameter, PowerShell automatically prompts him for it. When not specified, the parameter is optional.

`Position = `*`position`*

Defines the position of this parameter. This applies when the user provides parameter values without specifying the parameter they apply to (e.g., *Argument2* in `Invoke-MyFunction `*`-Param1 Argument1 Argument2`*). PowerShell supplies these values to parameters that have defined a

`Position`, from lowest to highest. When not specified, the name of this parameter must be supplied by the user.

`ParameterSetName = `*`name`*

Defines this parameter as a member of a set of other related parameters. Parameter behavior for this parameter is then specific to this related set of parameters, and the parameter exists only in the parameter sets that it is defined in. This feature is used, for example, when the user may supply only a Name *or* ID. To include a parameter in two or more specific parameter sets, use two or more `[Parameter()]` attributes. When not specified, this parameter is a member of all parameter sets.

`ValueFromPipeline = $true`

Declares this parameter as one that directly accepts pipeline input. If the user pipes data into your script or function, PowerShell assigns this input to your parameter in your command's `process {}` block. When not specified, this parameter does not accept pipeline input directly.

`ValueFromPipelineByPropertyName = $true`

Declares this parameter as one that accepts pipeline input if a property of an incoming object matches its name. If this is true, PowerShell assigns the value of that property to your parameter in your command's `process {}` block. When not specified, this parameter does not accept pipeline input by property name.

`ValueFromRemainingArguments = $true`

Declares this parameter as one that accepts all remaining input that has not otherwise been assigned to positional or named parameters. Only one parameter can have this element. If no parameter declares support for this capability, PowerShell generates an error for arguments that cannot be assigned.

Parameter validation attributes

In addition to the [Parameter()] attribute, PowerShell lets you apply other attributes that add behavior or validation constraints to your parameters (all validation attributes are optional):

[Alias("*name*")]
> Defines an alternate name for this parameter. This is especially helpful for long parameter names that are descriptive but have a more common colloquial term. When not specified, the parameter can be referred to only by the name you originally declared.

[AllowNull()]
> Allows this parameter to receive $null as its value. This is required only for mandatory parameters. When not specified, mandatory parameters cannot receive $null as their value, although optional parameters can.

[AllowEmptyString()]
> Allows this string parameter to receive an empty string as its value. This is required only for mandatory parameters. When not specified, mandatory string parameters cannot receive an empty string as their value, although optional string parameters can. You can apply this to parameters that are not strings, but it has no impact.

[AllowEmptyCollection()]
> Allows this collection parameter to receive an empty collection as its value. This is required only for mandatory parameters. When not specified, mandatory collection parameters cannot receive an empty collection as their value, although optional collection parameters can. You can apply this to parameters that are not collections, but it has no impact.

[ValidateCount(*lower limit, upper limit*)]
> Restricts the number of elements that can be in a collection supplied to this parameter. When not specified, mandatory parameters have a lower limit of one element.

Optional parameters have no restrictions. You can apply this to parameters that are not collections, but it has no impact.

`[ValidateLength(lower limit, upper limit)]`

Restricts the length of strings that this parameter can accept. When not specified, mandatory parameters have a lower limit of one character. Optional parameters have no restrictions. You can apply this to parameters that are not strings, but it has no impact.

`[ValidatePattern("regular expression")]`

Enforces a pattern that input to this string parameter must match. When not specified, string inputs have no pattern requirements. You can apply this to parameters that are not strings, but it has no impact.

`[ValidateRange(lower limit, upper limit)]`

Restricts the upper and lower limit of numerical arguments that this parameter can accept. When not specified, parameters have no range limit. You can apply this to parameters that are not numbers, but it has no impact.

`[ValidateScript( { script block } )]`

Ensures that input supplied to this parameter satisfies the condition that you supply in the script block. PowerShell assigns the proposed input to the `$_` (or `$PSItem`) variable, and then invokes your script block. If the script block returns `$true` (or anything that can be converted to `$true`, such as nonempty strings), PowerShell considers the validation to have been successful.

`[ValidateSet("First Option", "Second Option", ..., "Last Option")]`

Ensures that input supplied to this parameter is equal to one of the options in the set. PowerShell uses its standard meaning of equality during this comparison: the same rules used by the `-eq` operator. If your validation requires nonstandard rules (such as case-sensitive comparison of strings), you can instead write the validation in the body of the script or function.

[ValidateNotNull()]

Ensures that input supplied to this parameter is not null. This is the default behavior of mandatory parameters, so this is useful only for optional parameters. When applied to string parameters, a $null parameter value gets instead converted to an empty string.

[ValidateNotNullOrEmpty()]

Ensures that input supplied to this parameter is not null or empty. This is the default behavior of mandatory parameters, so this is useful only for optional parameters. When applied to string parameters, the input must be a string with a length greater than one. When applied to collection parameters, the collection must have at least one element. When applied to other types of parameters, this attribute is equivalent to the [ValidateNotNull()] attribute.

Pipeline input

To access the data being passed to your command via the pipeline, use the input enumerator that PowerShell places in the $input special variable:

```
foreach($element in $input)
{
    "Input was: $element"
}
```

The $input variable is a .NET enumerator over the pipeline input. Enumerators support streaming scenarios very efficiently but do not let you access arbitrary elements as you would with an array. If you want to process their elements again, you must call the Reset() method on the $input enumerator once you reach the end.

If you need to access the pipeline input in an unstructured way, use the following command to convert the input enumerator to an array:

```
$inputArray = @($input)
```

Cmdlet keywords in commands

When pipeline input is a core scenario of your command, you
can include statement blocks labeled begin, process, and end:

```
param(...)

begin
{
    ...
}
process
{
    ...
}
end
{
    ...
}
```

PowerShell executes the begin statement when it loads your
command, the process statement for each item passed down
the pipeline, and the end statement after all pipeline input has
been processed. In the process statement block, the $_ (or
$PSItem) variable represents the current pipeline object.

When you write a command that includes these keywords, all
the commands in your script must be contained within the
statement blocks.

$MyInvocation automatic variable

The $MyInvocation automatic variable contains information
about the context under which the script was run, including
detailed information about the command (*MyCommand*), the
script that defines it (*ScriptName*), and more.

Retrieving Output from Commands

PowerShell provides three primary ways to retrieve output
from a command.

Pipeline output

any command

The return value/output of a script is any data that it generates but does not capture. If a command contains:

```
"Text Output"
5*5
```

then assigning the output of that command to a variable creates an array with the two values Text Output and 25.

Return statement

```
return value
```

The statement:

```
return $false
```

is simply a short form for pipeline output:

```
$false
return
```

Exit statement

```
exit errorlevel
```

The exit statement returns an error code from the current command or instance of PowerShell. If called anywhere in a script (inline, in a function, or in a script block), it exits the script. If called outside of a script (for example, a function), it exits PowerShell. The exit statement sets the $LastExitCode automatic variable to *errorlevel*. In turn, that sets the $? automatic variable to $false if *errorlevel* is not zero.

NOTE

Type **Get-Help about_automatic_variables** for more information about automatic variables.

Managing Errors

PowerShell supports two classes of errors: *nonterminating* and *terminating*. It collects both types of errors as a list in the $error automatic variable.

Nonterminating Errors

Most errors are *nonterminating errors*, in that they do not halt execution of the current cmdlet, script, function, or pipeline. When a command outputs an error (via PowerShell's error-output facilities), PowerShell writes that error to a stream called the *error output stream*.

You can output a nonterminating error using the Write-Error cmdlet (or the WriteError() API when writing a cmdlet).

The $ErrorActionPreference automatic variable lets you control how PowerShell handles nonterminating errors. It supports the following values, shown in Table 1-13.

Table 1-13. ErrorActionPreference automatic variable values

Value	Meaning
Ignore	Do not display errors, and do not add them to the $error collection. Only supported when supplied to the ErrorAction parameter of a command.
SilentlyContinue	Do not display errors, but add them to the $error collection.
Stop	Treat nonterminating errors as terminating errors.
Continue	Display errors, but continue execution of the current cmdlet, script, function, or pipeline. This is the default.
Inquire	Display a prompt that asks how PowerShell should treat this error.

Most cmdlets let you configure this explicitly by passing one of these values to the ErrorAction parameter.

Terminating Errors

A *terminating error* halts execution of the current cmdlet, script, function, or pipeline. If a command (such as a cmdlet or .NET method call) generates a structured exception (for example, if you provide a method with parameters outside their valid range), PowerShell exposes this as a terminating error. PowerShell also generates a terminating error if it fails to parse an element of your script, function, or pipeline.

You can generate a terminating error in your script using the throw keyword:

```
throw message
```

NOTE

In your own scripts and cmdlets, generate terminating errors only when the fundamental intent of the operation is impossible to accomplish. For example, failing to execute a command on a remote server should be considered a nonterminating error, whereas failing to connect to the remote server altogether should be considered a terminating error.

You can intercept terminating errors through the try, catch, and finally statements, as supported by many other programming languages:

```
try
{
    statement block
}
catch [exception type]
{
    error handling block
}
catch [alternate exception type]
```

```
{
    alternate error handling block
}
finally
{
    cleanup block
}
```

After a try statement, you must provide a catch statement, a finally statement, or both. If you specify an exception type (which is optional), you may specify more than one catch statement to handle exceptions of different types. If you specify an exception type, the catch block applies only to terminating errors of that type.

PowerShell also lets you intercept terminating errors if you define a trap statement before PowerShell encounters that error:

```
trap [exception type]
{
    statement block
    [continue or break]
}
```

If you specify an exception type, the trap statement applies only to terminating errors of that type.

Within a catch block or trap statement, the $_ (or $PSItem) variable represents the current exception or error being processed.

If specified, the continue keyword tells PowerShell to continue processing your script, function, or pipeline after the point at which it encountered the terminating error.

If specified, the break keyword tells PowerShell to halt processing the rest of your script, function, or pipeline after the point at which it encountered the terminating error. The default mode is break, and it applies if you specify neither break nor continue.

Formatting Output

Pipeline | Formatting Command

When objects reach the end of the output pipeline, PowerShell converts them to text to make them suitable for human consumption. PowerShell supports several options to help you control this formatting process, as listed in Table 1-14.

Table 1-14. PowerShell formatting commands

Formatting command	Result
Format-Table	Formats the properties of the input objects as a table, including only the object properties you specify. If you do not specify a property list, PowerShell picks a default set. In addition to supplying object properties, you may also provide advanced formatting statements:

```
PS > Get-Process | `
   Format-Table -Auto Name,`
   @{Label="HexId";
     Expression={ "{0:x}" -f $_.Id}
     Width=4
     Align="Right"
     }
```

The advanced formatting statement is a hashtable with the keys Label and Expression (or any short form of them). The value of the expression key should be a script block that returns a result for the current object (represented by the $_ variable).

For more information about the Format-Table cmdlet, type **Get-Help Format-Table**.

Formatting command	Result
Format-List	Formats the properties of the input objects as a list, including only the object properties you specify. If you do not specify a property list, PowerShell picks a default set. The Format-List cmdlet supports advanced formatting statements as used by the Format-Table cmdlet.
	The Format-List cmdlet is the one you will use most often to get a detailed summary of an object's properties. The command Format-List * returns all properties, but it does not include those that PowerShell hides by default. The command Format-List * -Force returns all properties.
	For more information about the Format-List cmdlet, type **Get-Help Format-List**.
Format-Wide	Formats the properties of the input objects in an extremely terse summary view. If you do not specify a property, PowerShell picks a default.
	In addition to supplying object properties, you can also provide advanced formatting statements:
	``PS > Get-Process	`    Format-Wide -Auto ` @{ Expression={ "{0:x}" -f $_.Id} }```
	The advanced formatting statement is a hashtable with the key Expression (or any short form of it). The value of the expression key should be a script block that returns a result for the current object (represented by the $_ variable).
	For more information about the Format-Wide cmdlet, type **Get-Help Format-Wide**.

Custom Formatting Files

All the formatting defaults in PowerShell (for example, when you do not specify a formatting command, or when you do not specify formatting properties) are driven by the *.Format.Ps1Xml* files in the installation directory.

To create your own formatting customizations, use these files as a source of examples, but do not modify them directly. Instead, create a new file and use the Update-FormatData cmdlet to load your customizations. The Update-FormatData cmdlet applies your changes to the current instance of PowerShell. If you wish to load them every time you launch PowerShell, call Update-FormatData in your profile script. The following command loads *Format.custom.ps1xml* from the same directory as your profile:

```
$formatFile = Join-Path (Split-Path $profile)
    "Format.Custom.Ps1Xml"
Update-FormatData -PrependPath $formatFile
```

Capturing Output

There are several ways to capture the output of commands in PowerShell, as listed in Table 1-15.

Table 1-15. Capturing output in PowerShell

Command	Result
$variable = Command	Stores the objects produced by the PowerShell command into $variable.
$variable = Command | Out-String	Stores the visual representation of the PowerShell command into $variable. This is the PowerShell command after it's been converted to human-readable output.
$variable = NativeCommand	Stores the (string) output of the native command into $variable. PowerShell stores this as a list of strings—one for each line of output from the native command.

Command	Result
Command -OutVariable *variable*	For most commands, stores the objects produced by the PowerShell command into $*variable*. The parameter -OutVariable can also be written -Ov.
Command > *File*	Redirects the visual representation of the PowerShell (or standard output of a native command) into *File*, overwriting *File* if it exists. Errors are not captured by this redirection.
Command >> *File*	Redirects the visual representation of the PowerShell (or standard output of a native command) into *File*, appending to *File* if it exists. Errors are not captured by this redirection.
Command 2> *File*	Redirects the errors from the PowerShell or native command into *File*, overwriting *File* if it exists.
Command n>*File*	Redirects stream number *n* into *File*, overwriting *File* if it exists. Supported streams are 2 for error, 3 for warning, 4 for verbose, 5 for debug, 6 for the structured information stream, and * for all.
Command 2>> *File*	Redirects the errors from the PowerShell or native command into *File*, appending to *File* if it exists.
Command n>> *File*	Redirects stream number *n* into *File*, appending to *File* if it exists. Supported streams are 2 for error, 3 for warning, 4 for verbose, 5 for debug, 6 for the structured information stream, and * for all.

Command	Result
Command > *File* 2>&1	Redirects both the error and standard output streams of the PowerShell or native command into *File*, overwriting *File* if it exists.
Command >> *File* 2>&1	Redirects both the error and standard output streams of the PowerShell or native command into *File*, appending to *File* if it exists.

While output from the Write-Host cmdlet normally goes directly to the screen, you can use the structured information stream to capture it into a variable:

```
PS > function HostWriter { Write-Host "Console Output" }
PS > $a = HostWriter
Console Output
PS > $a
PS > $a = HostWriter 6>&1
PS > $a
Console Output
```

Common Customization Points

As useful as it is out of the box, PowerShell offers several avenues for customization and personalization.

Console Settings

The Windows PowerShell user interface offers several features to make your shell experience more efficient.

Adjust your font size

Both the Windows Terminal application and the default Windows Console let you adjust font size.

To temporarily change your font size, hold down the Ctrl key and use the mouse to scroll up or down. In the Windows Terminal application, you can also use the Ctrl+Plus or Ctrl

+Minus hotkeys. In the Windows Terminal application, Ctrl+0 resets the font size back to your default.

To change your font size default in the default Windows Console, open the System menu (right-click the title bar at the top left of the console window), select Properties→Font. If you launch Windows PowerShell from the Start menu, it launches with some default modifications to the font and window size. To change your font size default in the Windows Terminal application, add a fontSize setting to any of your terminal profiles:

```
{
    "guid": "...",
    "name": "PowerShell (Demos)",
    "fontSize": 18,
    "colorScheme": "Campbell Powershell",
    "source": "Windows.Terminal.PowershellCore"
},
```

Adjust other Windows Terminal settings

The Windows Terminal application includes a wealth of configuration settings. A sample of these include:

- Configuring the list of available shells and applications (such as bash.exe)
- Color schemes and user interface themes
- Binding actions to hotkeys
- Text selection behavior
- Window transparency
- Background images

For a full list of these, see the documentation for global settings (*https://aka.ms/terminal-global-settings*) and general profile settings (*https://aka.ms/terminal-profile-settings*) in Windows Terminal.

Use hotkeys to operate the shell more efficiently

The PowerShell console supports many hotkeys that help make operating the console more efficient, as shown in Table 1-16.

Table 1-16. PowerShell hotkeys

Hotkey	Meaning
Press and release the Windows key, and then type **pwsh** or **power shell**	Launch PowerShell or Windows PowerShell. The Win+X hotkey also provides a quick way to launch Windows PowerShell.
Up arrow	Scan backward through your command history.
Down arrow	Scan forward through your command history.
Left arrow	Move cursor one character to the left on your command line.
Right arrow	Move cursor one character to the right on your command line. If at the end of the line, inserts a character from the text of your last command at that position.
Ctrl+Left arrow	Move the cursor one word to the left on your command line.
Ctrl+Right arrow	Move the cursor one word to the right on your command line.
Home	Move the cursor to the beginning of the command line.
End	Move the cursor to the end of the command line.
Ctrl+Shift+PgUp, Ctrl+Shift+PgDn	In the Windows Terminal application, scroll through the screen buffer. In the Windows Console, you can use PgUp and PgDn.
Ctrl+Shift+F	In the Windows Terminal application, searches for text in the screen buffer. In the Windows Console, you can use Alt+Space E F.
Alt+Space E K	In the Windows Console, selects text to be copied from the screen buffer.

Hotkey	Meaning
Ctrl+C	Cancel the current operation. If any text is selected, Ctrl+C copies this text into the clipboard.
Ctrl+V	Paste clipboard contents.
Ctrl+Shift+T	In the Windows Terminal application, opens a new tab. You can also use Ctrl+Shift+1, Ctrl+Shift+2, and similar to open a tab for that numbered profile (such as bash.exe).
Ctrl+Shift+W, Alt+F4	In the Windows Terminal application, close the current tab or entire application. In the Windows Console, you can use Alt+Space C to close the entire application.
Ctrl+Break	In the Windows Console, breaks the PowerShell debugger into the currently running script.
Ctrl+Home	Deletes characters from the beginning of the current command line up to (but not including) the current cursor position.
Ctrl+End	Deletes characters from (and including) the current cursor position to the end of the current command line.
Ctrl+Z, Ctrl+Y	Undo and Redo.
F8	Scan backward through your command history, only displaying matches for commands that match the text you've typed so far on the command line.
Ctrl+R	Begins an interactive search backward through your command history based on text you type interactively.

NOTE

The command-line editing experience offered in PowerShell through the PSReadLine module is far richer than what this table lists. It includes Emacs and Vi key bindings, as well as the ability to define your own— you can see the full default list by typing **Get-PSReadLineKeyHandler**.

Profiles

PowerShell automatically runs the four scripts listed in Table 1-17 during startup. Each, if present, lets you customize your execution environment. PowerShell runs anything you place in these files as though you had entered it manually at the command line.

Table 1-17. PowerShell profiles

Profile purpose	Profile location
Customization of all PowerShell sessions, including PowerShell hosting applications for all users on the system	*InstallationDirectory\profile.ps1*
Customization of *pwsh.exe* sessions for all users on the system	*InstallationDirectory \Microsoft.PowerShell_profile.ps1*
Customization of all PowerShell sessions, including PowerShell hosting applications	*<My Documents>\PowerShell \profile.ps1*
Typical customization of *pwsh.exe* sessions	*<My Documents>\PowerShell \Microsoft.PowerShell_profile.ps1*

In Windows PowerShell, some of these locations will be different.

PowerShell makes editing your profile script simple by defining the automatic variable $profile. By itself, it points to the "current user, pwsh.exe" profile. In addition, the $profile variable defines additional properties that point to the other profile locations:

```
PS > $profile | Format-List -Force

AllUsersAllHosts       : C:\...Microsoft.PowerShell..\profile.ps1
AllUsersCurrentHost    : C:\...\Microsoft.PowerShell_profile.ps1
CurrentUserAllHosts    : D:\Lee\PowerShell\profile.ps1
CurrentUserCurrentHost : D:\...\Microsoft.PowerShell_profile.ps1
```

To create a new profile, type:

```
New-Item -Type file -Force $profile
```

To edit this profile, type:

```
notepad $profile
```

Prompts

To customize your prompt, add a prompt function to your profile. This function returns a string. For example:

```
function prompt
{
    "PS [$env:COMPUTERNAME] >"
}
```

Tab Completion

You can define a TabExpansion2 function to customize the way that PowerShell completes properties, variables, parameters, and files when you press the Tab key.

Your TabExpansion function overrides the one that PowerShell defines by default, though, so you may want to use its definition as a starting point:

```
Get-Content function:\TabExpansion2
```

User Input

You can define a PSConsoleHostReadLine function to customize the way that the PowerShell console host (not the Integrated Scripting Environment [ISE]) reads input from the user. This function is responsible for handling all of the user's keypresses, and finally returning the command that PowerShell should invoke.

Command Resolution

You can intercept PowerShell's command resolution behavior in three places by assigning a script block to one or all of the PreCommandLookupAction, PostCommandLookupAction, or Command NotFoundAction properties of $executionContext.Session State.InvokeCommand.

PowerShell invokes the PreCommandLookupAction after the user types a command name, but before it has tried to resolve the command. It invokes the PostCommandLookupAction once it has resolved a command, but before it executes the command. It invokes the CommandNotFoundAction when a command is not found, but before it generates an error message. Each script block receives two arguments—CommandName and Command LookupEventArgs:

```
$executionContext.SessionState.
    InvokeCommand.CommandNotFoundAction = {
        param($CommandName,
    $CommandLookupEventArgs)
        (...)
}
```

If your script block assigns a script block to the CommandScript Block property of the CommandLookupEventArgs or assigns a CommandInfo to the Command property of the CommandLookup EventArgs, PowerShell will use that script block or command, respectively. If your script block sets the StopSearch property to true, PowerShell will do no further command resolution.

## CHAPTER 2

Regular Expression Reference

Regular expressions play an important role in most text parsing and text matching tasks. They form an important underpinning of the -split and -match operators, the switch statement, the Select-String cmdlet, and more. Tables 2-1 through 2-10 list commonly used regular expressions.

Table 2-1. Character classes: patterns that represent sets of characters

Character class	Matches

.	Any character except for a newline. If the regular expression uses the SingleLine option, it matches any character.
	```PS > "T" -match '.'```
	```True```

[*characters*]	Any character in the brackets. For example: [aeiou].
	```PS > "Test" -match '[Tes]'```
	```True```

[^*characters*]	Any character not in the brackets. For example: [^aeiou].
	```PS > "Test" -match '[^Tes]'```
	```False```

Character class	Matches
[*start-end*]	Any character between the characters *start* and *end*, inclusive. You may include multiple character ranges between the brackets. For example, [a-eh-j]. PS > "Test" -match '[e-t]' True
[^*start-end*]	Any character not between any of the character ranges *start* through *end*, inclusive. You may include multiple character ranges between the brackets. For example, [^a-eh-j]. PS > "Test" -match '[^e-t]' False
\p{*character class*}	Any character in the Unicode group or block range specified by {*character class*}. PS > "+" -match '\p{Sm}' True
\P{*character class*}	Any character not in the Unicode group or block range specified by {*character class*}. PS > "+" -match '\P{Sm}' False
\w	Any word character. Note that this is the *Unicode* definition of a word character, which includes digits, as well as many math symbols and various other symbols. PS > "a" -match '\w' True
\W	Any nonword character. PS > "!" -match '\W' True

Character class	Matches

\s	Any whitespace character.
	```PS > "`t" -match '\s'```
	```True```

\S	Any nonwhitespace character.
	```PS > " `t" -match '\S'```
	```False```

\d	Any decimal digit.
	```PS > "5" -match '\d'```
	```True```

\D	Any character that isn't a decimal digit.
	```PS > "!" -match '\D'```
	```True```

Table 2-2. Quantifiers: expressions that enforce quantity on the preceding expression

Quantifier	Meaning

<none>	One match.
	```PS > "T" -match 'T'```
	```True```

*	Zero or more matches, matching as much as possible.
	```PS > "A" -match 'T*'```
	```True```
	```PS > "TTTTT" -match '^T*$'```
	```True```
	
	```PS > 'ATTT' -match 'AT*'; $Matches[0]```
	```True```
	```ATTT```

Quantifier	Meaning
+	One or more matches, matching as much as possible. ``` PS > "A" -match 'T+' False PS > "TTTTT" -match '^T+$' True PS > 'ATTT' -match 'AT+'; $Matches[0] True ATTT ```
?	Zero or one matches, matching as much as possible. ``` PS > "TTTTT" -match '^T?$' False PS > 'ATTT' -match 'AT?'; $Matches[0] True AT ```
{n}	Exactly n matches. ``` PS > "TTTTT" -match '^T{5}$' True ```
{n,}	n or more matches, matching as much as possible. ``` PS > "TTTTT" -match '^T{4,}$' True ```
{n,m}	Between n and m matches (inclusive), matching as much as possible. ``` PS > "TTTTT" -match '^T{4,6}$' True ```
*?	Zero or more matches, matching as little as possible. ``` PS > "A" -match '^AT*?$' True PS > 'ATTT' -match 'AT*?'; $Matches[0] True A ```

Quantifier	Meaning
+?	One or more matches, matching as little as possible.

	`PS > "A" -match '^AT+?$'`
	`False`
	
	`PS > 'ATTT' -match 'AT+?'; $Matches[0]`
	`True`
	`AT`

??	Zero or one matches, matching as little as possible.

	`PS > "A" -match '^AT??$'`
	`True`
	
	`PS > 'ATTT' -match 'AT??'; $Matches[0]`
	`True`
	`A`

{n}?	Exactly n matches.
	`PS > "TTTTT" -match '^T{5}?$'` `True`
{n,}?	n or more matches, matching as little as possible.
	`PS > "TTTTT" -match '^T{4,}?$'` `True`
{n,m}?	Between n and m matches (inclusive), matching as little as possible.
	`PS > "TTTTT" -match '^T{4,6}?$'` `True`

Table 2-3. Grouping constructs: expressions that let you group characters, patterns, and other expressions

Grouping construct	Description

(text)	Captures the text matched inside the parentheses. These captures are named by number (starting at one) based on the order of the opening parenthesis.
	`PS > "Hello" -match '^(.*)llo$';`
	`    $matches[1]`
	`True`
	`He`

Grouping construct	Description

(?<name>)	Captures the text matched inside the parentheses. These captures are named by the name given in *name*.
	
	```PS > "Hello" -match '^(?<One>.*)llo$';```
	``` $matches.One```
	```True```
	```He```

(?<name1-name2>)	A balancing group definition. This is an advanced regular expression construct, but lets you match evenly balanced pairs of terms.

(?:)	Noncapturing group.
	
	```PS > "A1" -match '((A|B)\d)'; $matches```
	```True```

```
Name                                Value
----                                -----
2                                   A
1                                   A1
0                                   A1
```

```
PS > "A1" -match '((?:A|B)\d)'; $matches
True
```

```
Name                                Value
----                                -----
1                                   A1
0                                   A1
```

(?*imnsx-imnsx*:)	Applies or disables the given option for this group. Supported options are:
	i case-insensitive
	m multiline
	n explicit capture
	s singleline
	x ignore whitespace
	
	```PS > "Te`nst" -match '(T e.st)'```
	```False```
	```PS > "Te`nst" -match '(?sx:T e.st)'```
	```True```

Grouping construct	Description
(?=)	Zero-width positive lookahead assertion. Ensures that the given pattern matches to the right, without actually performing the match. ``` PS > "555-1212" -match '(?=...-)(.*)'; $matches[1] True 555-1212 ```
(?!)	Zero-width negative lookahead assertion. Ensures that the given pattern does not match to the right, without actually performing the match. ``` PS > "friendly" -match '(?!friendly)friend' False ```

Table 2-4. More grouping constructs

Grouping construct	Description
(?<=)	Zero-width positive lookbehind assertion. Ensures that the given pattern matches to the left, without actually performing the match. ``` PS > "public int X" -match '^.*(?<=public)int .*$' True ```
(?<!)	Zero-width negative lookbehind assertion. Ensures that the given pattern does not match to the left, without actually performing the match. ``` PS > "private int X" -match '^.*(?<!private)int .*$' False ```
(?>)	Nonbacktracking subexpression. Matches only if this subexpression can be matched completely. ``` PS > "Hello World" -match '(Hello.*)orld' True PS > "Hello World" -match '(?>Hello.*)orld' False ``` The nonbacktracking version of the subexpression fails to match, as its complete match would be "Hello World".

Table 2-5. Atomic zero-width assertions: patterns that restrict where a match may occur

Assertion	Restriction
^	The match must occur at the beginning of the string (or line, if the Multiline option is in effect). PS > "Test" -match '^est' False
$	The match must occur at the end of the string (or line, if the Multiline option is in effect). PS > "Test" -match 'Tes$' False
\A	The match must occur at the beginning of the string. PS > "The`nTest" -match '(?m:^Test)' True PS > "The`nTest" -match '(?m:\ATest)' False
\Z	The match must occur at the end of the string, or before \n at the end of the string. PS > "The`nTest`n" -match '(?m:The$)' True PS > "The`nTest`n" -match '(?m:The\Z)' False PS > "The`nTest`n" -match 'Test\Z' True
\z	The match must occur at the end of the string. PS > "The`nTest`n" -match 'Test\z' False
\G	The match must occur where the previous match ended. Used with System.Text.RegularExpressions.Match.NextMatch()
\b	The match must occur on a word boundary: the first or last characters in words separated by nonalphanumeric characters. PS > "Testing" -match 'ing\b' True

Assertion	Restriction
\B	The match must not occur on a word boundary. PS > "Testing" -match 'ing\B' False

Table 2-6. Substitution patterns: patterns used in a regular expression replace operation

Pattern	Substitution
$*number*	The text matched by group number *number*. PS > "Test" -replace "(.*)st",'$1ar' Tear

${*name*}	The text matched by group named *name*.
	PS > "Test" -replace "(?<pre>.*)st",'${pre}ar'
	Tear

$$	A literal $. PS > "Test" -replace ".",'$$' $$$$
$&	A copy of the entire match. PS > "Test" -replace "^.*$",'Found: $&' Found: Test
$`	The text of the input string that precedes the match. PS > "Test" -replace "est$",'Te$`' TTeT
$'	The text of the input string that follows the match. PS > "Test" -replace "^Tes",'Res$''' Restt
$+	The last group captured. PS > "Testing" -replace "(.*)ing",'$+ed' Tested
$_	The entire input string. PS > "Testing" -replace "(.*)ing",'String: $_' String: Testing

Table 2-7. Alternation constructs: expressions that let you perform either/or logic

Alternation construct	Description

|	Matches any of the terms separated by the vertical bar character.
	```PS > "Test" -match '(B|T)est'```
	```True```

(?(*expression*)
yes|*no*)
	Matches the *yes term* if expression matches at this point. Otherwise, matches the *no term*. The *no term* is optional.
	```PS > "3.14" -match '(?(\d)3.14|Pi)'```
	```True```
	```PS > "Pi" -match '(?(\d)3.14|Pi)'```
	```True```
	```PS > "2.71" -match '(?(\d)3.14|Pi)'```
	```False```

(?(*name*)*yes*|
no)
	Matches the *yes term* if the capture group named name has a capture at this point. Otherwise, matches the *no term*. The *no term* is optional.
	```PS > "123" -match '(?<one>1)?(?(one)23|234)'```
	```True```
	```PS > "23" -match '(?<one>1)?(?(one)23|234)'```
	```False```
	```PS > "234" -match '(?<one>1)?(?(one)23|234)'```
	```True```

Table 2-8. Backreference constructs: expressions that refer to a capture group within the expression

Backreference construct	Refers to

number	Group number *number* in the expression.
	```PS > "|Text|" -match '(.)Text\1'```
	```True```
	```PS > "|Text+" -match '(.)Text\1'```
	```False```

Backreference construct	Refers to
\k<*name*>	The group named *name* in the expression.

	```PS > "|Text|" -match '(?<Symbol>.)Text\k<Symbol>'```
	True
	```PS > "|Text+" -match '(?<Symbol>.)Text\k<Symbol>'```
	False

Table 2-9. Other constructs: other expressions that modify a regular expression

Construct	Description
(?*imnsx-imnsx*)	Applies or disables the given option for the rest of this expression. Supported options are: i case-insensitive m multiline n explicit capture s singleline x ignore whitespace ```PS > "Te`nst" -match '(?sx)T e.st'``` True
(?#)	Inline comment. This terminates at the first closing parenthesis. ```PS > "Test" -match '(?# Match "Test")Test'``` True
# *[to end of line]*	Comment form allowed when the regular expression has the IgnoreWhitespace option enabled. ```PS > "Test" -match '(?x)Test # Matches Test'``` True

Table 2-10. Character escapes: character sequences that represent another character

Escaped character	Match
`<ordinary characters>`	Characters other than . $ ^ { [(	) * + ? \ match themselves.
`\a`	A bell (alarm) \u0007.
`\b`	A backspace \u0008 if in a [ ] character class. In a regular expression, \b denotes a word boundary (between \w and \W characters) except within a [ ] character class, where \b refers to the backspace character. In a replacement pattern, \b always denotes a backspace.
`\t`	A tab \u0009.
`\r`	A carriage return \u000D.
`\v`	A vertical tab \u000B.
`\f`	A form feed \u000C.
`\n`	A new line \u000A.
`\e`	An escape \u001B.
`\ddd`	An ASCII character as octal (up to three digits). Numbers with no leading zero are treated as backreferences if they have only one digit, or if they correspond to a capturing group number.
`\xdd`	An ASCII character using hexadecimal representation (exactly two digits).
`\cC`	An ASCII control character; for example, \cC is Control-C.
`\udddd`	A Unicode character using hexadecimal representation (exactly four digits).
`\`	When followed by a character that is not recognized as an escaped character, matches that character. For example, * is the literal character *.

## CHAPTER 3

XPath Quick Reference

Just as regular expressions are the standard way to interact with plain text, XPath is the standard way to interact with XML. Because of that, XPath is something you're likely to run across in your travels. Several cmdlets support XPath queries: Select-Xml, Get-WinEvent, and more. Tables 3-1 and 3-2 give a quick overview of XPath concepts.

For these examples, consider this sample XML:

```
<AddressBook>
  <Person contactType="Personal">
    <Name>Lee</Name>
    <Phone type="home">555-1212</Phone>
    <Phone type="work">555-1213</Phone>
  </Person>
  <Person contactType="Business">
    <Name>Ariel</Name>
    <Phone>555-1234</Phone>
  </Person>
</AddressBook>
```

Table 3-1. Navigation and selection

Syntax	Meaning

/	Represents the root of the XML tree.
	For example:
	`PS > $xml | Select-Xml "/" |`
	`    Select -Expand Node`
	
	`AddressBook`
	`-----------`
	`AddressBook`

/Node	Navigates to the node named *Node* from the root of the XML tree.
	For example:
	`PS > $xml | Select-Xml "/AddressBook" |`
	`    Select -Expand Node`
	
	`Person`
	`------`
	`{Lee, Ariel}`

/Node/*/Node2	Navigates to the node named *Node2* via *Node*, allowing any single node in between.
	For example:
	`PS > $xml | Select-Xml "/AddressBook/*/Name" |`
	`    Select -Expand Node`
	
	`#text`
	`-----`
	`Lee`
	`Ariel`

//Node	Finds all nodes named *Node*, anywhere in the XML tree.
	For example:
	`PS > $xml | Select-Xml "//Phone" |`
	`    Select -Expand Node`
	
	`type      #text`
	`----      -----`
	`home      555-1212`
	`work      555-1213`
	`          555-1234`

Syntax	Meaning
..	Retrieves the parent node of the given node.

For example:

```
PS > $xml | Select-Xml "//Phone" |
    Select -Expand Node
```

type	#text
home	555-1212
work	555-1213
	555-1234

```
PS > $xml | Select-Xml "//Phone/.."|
    Select -Expand Node
```

contactType	Name	Phone
Personal	Lee	{Phone, Phone}
Business	Ariel	555-1234

Syntax	Meaning
@*Attribute*	Accesses the value of the attribute named *Attribute*.

For example:

```
PS > $xml | Select-Xml "//Phone/@type" |
    Select -Expand Node
```

#text
home
work

Table 3-2. Comparisons

Syntax	Meaning
[ ]	Filtering, similar to the `Where-Object` cmdlet. For example:

```
PS > $xml |
    Select-Xml "//Person[@contactType = 'Personal']" |
    Select -Expand Node

contactType            Name                 Phone
-----------            ----                 -----
Personal               Lee                  {Phone, Phone}


PS > $xml | Select-Xml "//Person[Name = 'Lee']" |
    Select -Expand Node

contactType            Name                 Phone
-----------            ----                 -----
Personal               Lee                  {Phone, Phone}
```

and	Logical *and*.
or	Logical *or*.
not()	Logical *negation*.
=	*Equality*.
!=	*Inequality*.

## CHAPTER 4

.NET String Formatting

String Formatting Syntax

The format string supported by the format (-f) operator is a string that contains format items. Each format item takes the form of:

{*index*[*,alignment*][*:formatString*]}

index represents the zero-based index of the item in the object array following the format operator.

alignment is optional and represents the alignment of the item. A positive number aligns the item to the right of a field of the specified width. A negative number aligns the item to the left of a field of the specified width:

```
PS > ("{0,6}" -f 4.99), ("{0,6:##.00}" -f 15.9)
  4.99
 15.90
```

formatString is optional and formats the item using that type's specific format string syntax (as laid out in Tables 4-1 and 4-2).

Standard Numeric Format Strings

Table 4-1 lists the standard numeric format strings. All format specifiers may be followed by a number between 0 and 99 to control the precision of the formatting.

Table 4-1. Standard numeric format strings

Format specifier	Name	Description

C or c	Currency	A currency amount:
		`PS > "{0:C}" -f 1.23`
		`$1.23`

D or d	Decimal	A decimal amount (for integral types). The precision specifier controls the minimum number of digits in the result:
		`PS > "{0:D4}" -f 2`
		`0002`

E or e	Scientific	Scientific (exponential) notation. The precision specifier controls the number of digits past the decimal point:
		`PS > "{0:E3}" -f [Math]::Pi`
		`3.142E+000`

F or f	Fixed-point	Fixed-point notation. The precision specifier controls the number of digits past the decimal point:
		`PS > "{0:F3}" -f [Math]::Pi`
		`3.142`

G or g	General	The most compact representation (between fixed-point and scientific) of the number. The precision specifier controls the number of significant digits:
		`PS > "{0:G3}" -f [Math]::Pi`
		`3.14`
		`PS > "{0:G3}" -f 1mb`
		`1.05E+06`

Format specifier	Name	Description

N or n	Number	The human-readable form of the number, which includes separators between number groups. The precision specifier controls the number of digits past the decimal point:
		`PS > "{0:N4}" -f 1mb`
		`1,048,576.0000`

P or p	Percent	The number (generally between 0 and 1) represented as a percentage. The precision specifier controls the number of digits past the decimal point:
		`PS > "{0:P4}" -f 0.67`
		`67.0000 %`

R or r	Roundtrip	The Single or Double number formatted with a precision that guarantees the string (when parsed) will result in the original number again:
		`PS > "{0:R}" -f (1mb/2.0)`
		`524288`
		`PS > "{0:R}" -f (1mb/9.0)`
		`116508.44444444444`

X or x	Hexadecimal	The number converted to a string of hexadecimal digits. The case of the specifier controls the case of the resulting hexadecimal digits. The precision specifier controls the minimum number of digits in the resulting string:
		`PS > "{0:X4}" -f 1324`
		`052C`

Custom Numeric Format Strings

You can use custom numeric strings, listed in Table 4-2, to format numbers in ways not supported by the standard format strings.

Table 4-2. Custom numeric format strings

Format specifier	Name	Description

0	Zero placeholder	Specifies the precision and width of a number string. Zeros not matched by digits in the original number are output as zeros:
		`PS > "{0:00.0}" -f 4.12341234`
		`04.1`

#	Digit placeholder	Specifies the precision and width of a number string. # symbols not matched by digits in the input number are not output:
		`PS > "{0:##.#}" -f 4.12341234`
		`4.1`

.	Decimal point	Determines the location of the decimal:
		`PS > "{0:##.#}" -f 4.12341234`
		`4.1`

,	Thousands separator	When placed between a zero or digit placeholder before the decimal point in a formatting string, adds the separator character between number groups:
		`PS > "{0:#,#.#}" -f 1234.121234`
		`1,234.1`

,	Number scaling	When placed before the literal (or implicit) decimal point in a formatting string, divides the input by 1,000. You can apply this format specifier more than once:
		`PS > "{0:##,,.000}" -f 1048576`
		`1.049`

%	Percentage placeholder	Multiplies the input by 100, and inserts the percent sign where shown in the format specifier:
		`PS > "{0:%##.000}" -f .68`
		`%68.000`

Format specifier	Name	Description

E0
E+0
E-0
e0
e+0
e-0
	Scientific notation	Displays the input in scientific notation. The number of zeros that follow the E define the minimum length of the exponent field:
		`PS > "{0:##.#E000}" -f 2.71828`
		`27.2E-001`

' text '
" text "
	Literal string	Inserts the provided text literally into the output without affecting formatting:
		`PS > "{0:#.00'##'}" -f 2.71828`
		`2.72##`

;	Section separator	Allows for conditional formatting.
		If your format specifier contains no section separators, the formatting statement applies to all input.
		If your format specifier contains one separator (creating two sections), the first section applies to positive numbers and zero, and the second section applies to negative numbers.
		If your format specifier contains two separators (creating three sections), the sections apply to positive numbers, negative numbers, and zero:
		`PS > "{0:POS;NEG;ZERO}" -f -14`
		`NEG`

Other	Other character	Inserts the provided text literally into the output without affecting formatting:
		`PS > "{0:$## Please}" -f 14`
		`$14 Please`

## CHAPTER 5

.NET DateTime Formatting

DateTime format strings convert a DateTime object to one of several standard formats, as listed in Table 5-1.

Table 5-1. Standard DateTime format strings

Format specifier	Name	Description
d	Short date	The culture's short date format: PS > "{0:d}" -f [DateTime] "01/23/4567" 1/23/4567
D	Long date	The culture's long date format: PS > "{0:D}" -f [DateTime] "01/23/4567" Friday, January 23, 4567
f	Full date/ short time	Combines the long date and short time format patterns: PS > "{0:f}" -f [DateTime] "01/23/4567" Friday, January 23, 4567 12:00 AM
F	Full date/ long time	Combines the long date and long time format patterns: PS > "{0:F}" -f [DateTime] "01/23/4567" Friday, January 23, 4567 12:00:00 AM
g	General date/ short time	Combines the short date and short time format patterns: PS > "{0:g}" -f [DateTime] "01/23/4567" 1/23/4567 12:00 AM

Format specifier	Name	Description

G	General date/long time	Combines the short date and long time format patterns:
		`PS > "{0:G}" -f [DateTime] "01/23/4567"`
		`1/23/4567 12:00:00 AM`

M or m	Month day	The culture's `MonthDay` format:
		`PS > "{0:M}" -f [DateTime] "01/23/4567"`
		`January 23`

o	Round-trip date/time	The date formatted with a pattern that guarantees the string (when parsed) will result in the original DateTime again:
		`PS > "{0:o}" -f [DateTime] "01/23/4567"`
		`4567-01-23T00:00:00.0000000`

R or r	RFC1123	The standard RFC1123 format pattern:
		`PS > "{0:R}" -f [DateTime] "01/23/4567"`
		`Fri, 23 Jan 4567 00:00:00 GMT`

s	Sortable	Sortable format pattern. Conforms to ISO 8601 and provides output suitable for sorting:
		`PS > "{0:s}" -f [DateTime] "01/23/4567"`
		`4567-01-23T00:00:00`

t	Short time	The culture's `ShortTime` format:
		`PS > "{0:t}" -f [DateTime] "01/23/4567"`
		`12:00 AM`

T	Long time	The culture's `LongTime` format:
		`PS > "{0:T}" -f [DateTime] "01/23/4567"`
		`12:00:00 AM`

u	Universal sortable	The culture's `UniversalSortable DateTime` format applied to the UTC equivalent of the input:
		`PS > "{0:u}" -f [DateTime] "01/23/4567"`
		`4567-01-23 00:00:00Z`

Format specifier	Name	Description
U	Universal	The culture's FullDateTime format applied to the UTC equivalent of the input: PS > "{0:U}" -f [DateTime] "01/23/4567" Friday, January 23, 4567 8:00:00 AM
Y or y	Year month	The culture's YearMonth format: PS > "{0:Y}" -f [DateTime] "01/23/4567" January, 4567

Custom DateTime Format Strings

You can use the custom DateTime format strings listed in Table 5-2 to format dates in ways not supported by the standard format strings.

NOTE

Single-character format specifiers are by default interpreted as a standard DateTime formatting string unless they are used with other formatting specifiers. Add the % character before them to have them interpreted as a custom format specifier.

Table 5-2. Custom DateTime format strings

Format specifier	Description
d	Day of the month as a number between 1 and 31. Represents single-digit days without a leading zero: PS > "{0:%d}" -f [DateTime] "01/02/4567" 2

Format specifier	Description
dd	Day of the month as a number between 1 and 31. Represents single-digit days with a leading zero: ```PS > "{0:dd}" -f` ` [DateTime] "01/02/4567"` `02```
ddd	Abbreviated name of the day of week: ```PS > "{0:ddd}" -f` ` [DateTime] "01/02/4567"` `Fri```
dddd	Full name of the day of the week: ```PS > "{0:dddd}" -f` ` [DateTime] "01/02/4567"` `Friday```
f	Most significant digit of the seconds fraction (milliseconds): ```PS > $date = Get-Date` `PS > $date.Millisecond` `93` `PS > "{0:%f}" -f $date` `0```
ff	Two most significant digits of the seconds fraction (milliseconds): ```PS > $date = Get-Date` `PS > $date.Millisecond` `93` `PS > "{0:ff}" -f $date` `09```
fff	Three most significant digits of the seconds fraction (milliseconds): ```PS > $date = Get-Date` `PS > $date.Millisecond` `93` `PS > "{0:fff}" -f $date` `093```

Format specifier	Description
ffff	Four most significant digits of the seconds fraction (milliseconds): ``` PS > $date = Get-Date PS > $date.Millisecond 93 PS > "{0:ffff}" -f $date 0937 ```
fffff	Five most significant digits of the seconds fraction (milliseconds): ``` PS > $date = Get-Date PS > $date.Millisecond 93 PS > "{0:fffff}" -f $date 09375 ```
ffffff	Six most significant digits of the seconds fraction (milliseconds): ``` PS > $date = Get-Date PS > $date.Millisecond 93 PS > "{0:ffffff}" -f $date 093750 ```
fffffff	Seven most significant digits of the seconds fraction (milliseconds): ``` PS > $date = Get-Date PS > $date.Millisecond 93 PS > "{0:fffffff}" -f $date 0937500 ```
F FF FFF (...) FFFFFFF	Most significant digit of the seconds fraction (milliseconds). When compared to the lowercase series of 'f' specifiers, displays nothing if the number is zero: ``` PS > "{0:|F FF FFF FFFF|}" -f [DateTime] "01/02/4567" | |---- ```

Format specifier	Description

%g or gg	Era (e.g., A.D.):
	```PS > "{0:gg}" -f [DateTime]```
	``` "01/02/4567"```
	A.D.

%h	Hours, as a number between 1 and 12. Single digits do not include a leading zero:
	```PS > "{0:%h}" -f```
	``` [DateTime] "01/02/4567 4:00pm"```
	4

hh	Hours, as a number between 01 and 12. Single digits include a leading zero. Note: this is interpreted as a standard DateTime formatting string unless used with other formatting specifiers:
	```PS > "{0:hh}" -f```
	``` [DateTime] "01/02/4567 4:00pm"```
	04

%H	Hours, as a number between 0 and 23. Single digits do not include a leading zero:
	```PS > "{0:%H}" -f```
	``` [DateTime] "01/02/4567 4:00pm"```
	16

HH	Hours, as a number between 00 and 23. Single digits include a leading zero:
	```PS > "{0:HH}" -f```
	``` [DateTime] "01/02/4567 4:00am"```
	04

K	DateTime.Kind specifier that corresponds to the kind (i.e., local, UTC, or unspecified) of input date:
	```PS > "{0:%K}" -f```
	``` [DateTime]::Now.ToUniversalTime()```
	Z

m	Minute, as a number between 0 and 59. Single digits do not include a leading zero: ```PS > "{0:%m}" -f [DateTime]::Now``` 7

Format specifier	Description

mm	Minute, as a number between 00 and 59. Single digits include a leading zero:
	```PS > "{0:mm}" -f [DateTime]::Now```
	```08```

M	Month, as a number between 1 and 12. Single digits do not include a leading zero:
	```PS > "{0:%M}" -f```
	``` [DateTime] "01/02/4567"```
	```1```

MM	Month, as a number between 01 and 12. Single digits include a leading zero:
	```PS > "{0:MM}" -f```
	``` [DateTime] "01/02/4567"```
	```01```

MMM	Abbreviated month name:
	```PS > "{0:MMM}" -f```
	``` [DateTime] "01/02/4567"```
	```Jan```

MMMM	Full month name:
	```PS > "{0:MMMM}" -f```
	``` [DateTime] "01/02/4567"```
	```January```

s	Seconds, as a number between 0 and 59. Single digits do not include a leading zero:
	```PS > $date = Get-Date```
	```PS > "{0:%s}" -f $date```
	```7```

ss	Seconds, as a number between 00 and 59. Single digits include a leading zero:
	```PS > $date = Get-Date```
	```PS > "{0:ss}" -f $date```
	```07```

Format specifier	Description
t	First character of the a.m./p.m. designator: ``` PS > $date = Get-Date PS > "{0:%t}" -f $date P ```
tt	a.m./p.m. designator: ``` PS > $date = Get-Date PS > "{0:tt}" -f $date PM ```
y	Year, in (at most) two digits: ``` PS > "{0:%y}" -f [DateTime] "01/02/4567" 67 ```
yy	Year, in (at most) two digits: ``` PS > "{0:yy}" -f [DateTime] "01/02/4567" 67 ```
yyy	Year, in (at most) four digits: ``` PS > "{0:yyy}" -f [DateTime] "01/02/4567" 4567 ```
yyyy	Year, in (at most) four digits: ``` PS > "{0:yyyy}" -f [DateTime] "01/02/4567" 4567 ```
yyyyy	Year, in (at most) five digits: ``` PS > "{0:yyyy}" -f [DateTime] "01/02/4567" 04567 ```
z	Signed time zone offset from GMT. Does not include a leading zero: ``` PS > "{0:%z}" -f [DateTime]::Now -8 ```

Format specifier	Description

zz	Signed time zone offset from GMT. Includes a leading zero:
	`PS > "{0:zz}" -f [DateTime]::Now`
	`-08`

zzz	Signed time zone offset from GMT, measured in hours and minutes:
	`PS > "{0:zzz}" -f [DateTime]::Now`
	`-08:00`

:	Time separator:
	`PS > "{0:y/m/d h:m:s}" -f`
	`    [DateTime] "01/02/4567 4:00pm"`
	`67/0/2 4:0:0`

/	Date separator:
	`PS > "{0:y/m/d h:m:s}" -f`
	`    [DateTime] "01/02/4567 4:00pm"`
	`67/0/2 4:0:0`

" text "
' text '
	Inserts the provided text literally into the output without affecting formatting:
	`PS > "{0:'Day: 'dddd}" -f`
	`    [DateTime]::Now`
	`Day: Monday`

%c	Syntax allowing for single-character custom formatting specifiers. The % sign is not added to the output:
	`PS > "{0:%h}" -f`
	`    [DateTime] "01/02/4567 4:00pm"`
	`4`

Other	Inserts the provided text literally into the output without affecting formatting:
	`PS > "{0:dddd!}" -f [DateTime]::Now`
	`Monday!`

## CHAPTER 6

Selected .NET Classes and Their Uses

Tables 6-1 through 6-16 provide pointers to types in the .NET Framework that usefully complement the functionality that PowerShell provides. For detailed descriptions and documentation, refer to the official documentation (*https://docs.micro soft.com/en-us*).

Table 6-1. PowerShell

Class	Description
System.Management. Automation.PSObject	Represents a PowerShell object to which you can add notes, properties, and more.

Table 6-2. Utility

Class	Description
System.DateTime	Represents an instant in time, typically expressed as a date and time of day.
System.Guid	Represents a globally unique identifier (GUID).

Class	Description
System.Math	Provides constants and static methods for trigonometric, logarithmic, and other common mathematical functions.
System.Random	Represents a pseudorandom number generator, a device that produces a sequence of numbers that meet certain statistical requirements for randomness.
System.Convert	Converts a base data type to another base data type.
System.Environment	Provides information about, and means to manipulate, the current environment and platform.
System.Console	Represents the standard input, output, and error streams for console applications.
System.Text.Regular Expressions.Regex	Represents an immutable regular expression.
System.Diagnostics.Debug	Provides a set of methods and properties that help debug your code.
System.Diagnostics.EventLog	Provides interaction with Windows event logs.
System.Diagnostics.Process	Provides access to local and remote processes and enables you to start and stop local system processes.
System.Diagnostics.Stopwatch	Provides a set of methods and properties that you can use to accurately measure elapsed time.

Class	Description
System.Media.SoundPlayer	Controls playback of a sound from a *.wav* file.

Table 6-3. Collections and object utilities

Class	Description
System.Array	Provides methods for creating, manipulating, searching, and sorting arrays, thereby serving as the base class for all arrays in the Common Language Runtime.
System.Enum	Provides the base class for enumerations.
System.String	Represents text as a series of Unicode characters.
System.Text.StringBuilder	Represents a mutable string of characters.
System.Collections. Specialized.OrderedDictionary	Represents a collection of key/value pairs that are accessible by the key or index.
System.Collections.ArrayList	Implements the IList interface using an array whose size is dynamically increased as required.

Table 6-4. The .NET Framework

Class	Description
System.AppDomain	Represents an application domain, which is an isolated environment where applications execute.

Class	Description
System.Reflection.Assembly	Defines an Assembly, which is a reusable, versionable, and self-describing building block of a Common Language Runtime application.
System.Type	Represents type declarations: class types, interface types, array types, value types, enumeration types, type parameters, generic type definitions, and open or closed constructed generic types.
System.Threading.Thread	Creates and controls a thread, sets its priority, and gets its status.
System.Runtime.Interop Services.Marshal	Provides a collection of methods for allocating unmanaged memory, copying unmanaged memory blocks, and converting managed to unmanaged types, as well as other miscellaneous methods used when interacting with unmanaged code.
Microsoft.CSharp.CSharpCode Provider	Provides access to instances of the C# code generator and code compiler.

Table 6-5. Registry

Class	Description
Microsoft.Win32.Registry	Provides RegistryKey objects that represent the root keys in the local and remote Windows Registry and static methods to access key/value pairs.
Microsoft.Win32.RegistryKey	Represents a key-level node in the Windows Registry.

Table 6-6. Input and Output

Class	Description
System.IO.Stream	Provides a generic view of a sequence of bytes.
System.IO.BinaryReader	Reads primitive data types as binary values.
System.IO.BinaryWriter	Writes primitive types in binary to a stream.
System.IO.BufferedStream	Adds a buffering layer to read and write operations on another stream.
System.IO.Directory	Exposes static methods for creating, moving, and enumerating through directories and subdirectories.
System.IO.FileInfo	Provides instance methods for creating, copying, deleting, moving, and opening files, and aids in the creation of FileStream objects.
System.IO.DirectoryInfo	Exposes instance methods for creating, moving, and enumerating through directories and subdirectories.
System.IO.File	Provides static methods for creating, copying, deleting, moving, and opening files, and aids in the creation of FileStream objects.
System.IO.MemoryStream	Creates a stream whose backing store is memory.

Class	Description
`System.IO.Path`	Performs operations on `String` instances that contain file or directory path information. These operations are performed in a cross-platform manner.
`System.IO.TextReader`	Represents a reader that can read a sequential series of characters.
`System.IO.StreamReader`	Implements a `TextReader` that reads characters from a byte stream in a particular encoding.
`System.IO.TextWriter`	Represents a writer that can write a sequential series of characters.
`System.IO.StreamWriter`	Implements a `TextWriter` for writing characters to a stream in a particular encoding.
`System.IO.StringReader`	Implements a `TextReader` that reads from a string.
`System.IO.StringWriter`	Implements a `TextWriter` for writing information to a string.
`System.IO.Compression.Deflate Stream`	Provides methods and properties used to compress and decompress streams using the Deflate algorithm.
`System.IO.Compression.GZip Stream`	Provides methods and properties used to compress and decompress streams using the GZip algorithm.
`System.IO.FileSystemWatcher`	Listens to the filesystem change notifications and raises events when a directory or file in a directory changes.

Table 6-7. Security

Class	Description
System.Security.Principal. WindowsIdentity	Represents a Windows user.
System.Security.Principal. WindowsPrincipal	Allows code to check the Windows group membership of a Windows user.
System.Security.Principal. WellKnownSidType	Defines a set of commonly used security identifiers (SIDs).
System.Security.Principal. WindowsBuiltInRole	Specifies common roles to be used with IsInRole.
System.Security.SecureString	Represents text that should be kept confidential. The text is encrypted for privacy when being used and deleted from computer memory when no longer needed.
System.Security.Cryptography. TripleDESCryptoServiceProvider	Defines a wrapper object to access the cryptographic service provider (CSP) version of the TripleDES algorithm.
System.Security.Cryptography. PasswordDeriveBytes	Derives a key from a password using an extension of the PBKDF1 algorithm.
System.Security.Cryptography. SHA1	Computes the SHA1 hash for the input data.
System.Security.Access Control.FileSystemSecurity	Represents the access control and audit security for a file or directory.
System.Security.Access Control.RegistrySecurity	Represents the Windows access control security for a registry key.

Table 6-8. User interface

Class	Description
System.Windows.Forms.Form	Represents a window or dialog box that makes up an application's user interface.
System.Windows.Forms.Flow LayoutPanel	Represents a panel that dynamically lays out its contents.

Table 6-9. Image manipulation

Class	Description
System.Drawing.Image	A class that provides functionality for the Bitmap and Metafile classes.
System.Drawing.Bitmap	Encapsulates a GDI+ bitmap, which consists of the pixel data for a graphics image and its attributes. A bitmap is an object used to work with images defined by pixel data.

Table 6-10. Networking

Class	Description
System.Uri	Provides an object representation of a uniform resource identifier (URI) and easy access to the parts of the URI.
System.Net.NetworkCredential	Provides credentials for password-based authentication schemes such as basic, digest, Kerberos authentication, and NTLM.
System.Net.Dns	Provides simple domain name resolution functionality.
System.Net.FtpWebRequest	Implements a File Transfer Protocol (FTP) client.

Class	Description
System.Net.HttpWebRequest	Provides an HTTP-specific implementation of the WebRequest class.
System.Net.WebClient	Provides common methods for sending data to and receiving data from a resource identified by a URI.
System.Net.Sockets.TcpClient	Provides client connections for TCP network services.
System.Net.Mail.MailAddress	Represents the address of an electronic mail sender or recipient.
System.Net.Mail.MailMessage	Represents an email message that can be sent using the SmtpClient class.
System.Net.Mail.SmtpClient	Allows applications to send email by using the Simple Mail Transfer Protocol (SMTP).
System.IO.Ports.SerialPort	Represents a serial port resource.
System.Web.HttpUtility	Provides methods for encoding and decoding URLs when processing web requests.

Table 6-11. XML

Class	Description
System.Xml.XmlTextWriter	Represents a writer that provides a fast, noncached, forward-only way of generating streams or files containing XML data that conforms to the W3C Extensible Markup Language (XML) 1.0 and the namespaces in XML recommendations.
System.Xml.XmlDocument	Represents an XML document.

Table 6-12. Windows Management Instrumentation (WMI)

Class	Description
`System.Management.Management Object`	Represents a WMI instance.
`System.Management.Management Class`	Represents a management class. A management class is a WMI class such as `Win32_LogicalDisk` (which can represent a disk drive) or `Win32_Process` (which represents a process such as an instance of Notepad.exe). The members of this class enable you to access WMI data using a specific WMI class path. For more information, see "Win32 Classes" in the official Windows Management Instrumentation documentation (*https://aka.ms/wmi*).

Class	Description
`System.Management.Management ObjectSearcher`	Retrieves a collection of WMI management objects based on a specified query. This class is one of the more commonly used entry points to retrieving management information. For example, it can be used to enumerate all disk drives, network adapters, processes, and many more management objects on a system or to query for all network connections that are up, services that are paused, and so on. When instantiated, an instance of this class takes as input a WMI query represented in an `ObjectQuery` or its derivatives, and optionally a `ManagementScope` representing the WMI namespace to execute the query in. It can also take additional advanced options in an `EnumerationOptions`. When the `Get` method on this object is invoked, the `Management ObjectSearcher` executes the given query in the specified scope and returns a collection of management objects that match the query in a `Management ObjectCollection`.
`System.Management.Management DateTimeConverter`	Provides methods to convert DMTF datetime and time intervals to CLR-compliant `DateTime` and `TimeSpan` formats, and vice versa.

Class	Description
System.Management.Management EventWatcher	Subscribes to temporary event notifications based on a specified event query.

Table 6-13. Active Directory

Class	Description
System.DirectoryServices. DirectorySearcher	Performs queries against Active Directory.
System.DirectoryServices. DirectoryEntry	The DirectoryEntry class encapsulates a node or object in the Active Directory hierarchy.

Table 6-14. Database

Class	Description
System.Data.DataSet	Represents an in-memory cache of data.
System.Data.DataTable	Represents one table of in-memory data.
System.Data.SqlClient. SqlCommand	Represents a Transact-SQL statement or stored procedure to execute against a SQL Server database.
System.Data.SqlClient. SqlConnection	Represents an open connection to a SQL Server database.
System.Data.SqlClient. SqlDataAdapter	Represents a set of data commands and a database connection that are used to fill the DataSet and update a SQL Server database.
System.Data.Odbc.OdbcCommand	Represents a SQL statement or stored procedure to execute against a data source.

Class	Description
System.Data.Odbc.OdbcConnection	Represents an open connection to a data source.
System.Data.Odbc.OdbcDataAdapter	Represents a set of data commands and a connection to a data source that are used to fill the DataSet and update the data source.

Table 6-15. Message queuing

Class	Description
System.Messaging.MessageQueue	Provides access to a queue on a Message Queuing server.

Table 6-16. Transactions

Class	Description
System.Transactions.Transaction	Represents a transaction.

## CHAPTER 7

WMI Reference

The Windows Management Instrumentation (WMI) facilities in Windows offer thousands of classes that provide information of interest to administrators. Table 7-1 lists the categories and subcategories covered by WMI and can be used to get a general idea of the scope of WMI classes. Table 7-2 provides a selected subset of the most useful WMI classes. For more information about a category, search the official WMI documentation (*https://aka.ms/wmi*).

Table 7-1. WMI class categories and subcategories

Category	Subcategory
Computer system hardware	Cooling device, input device, mass storage, motherboard, controller and port, networking device, power, printing, telephony, video, and monitor
Operating system	COM, desktop, drivers, filesystem, job objects, memory and page files, multimedia audio/visual, networking, operating system events, operating system settings, processes, registry, scheduler jobs, security, services, shares, Start menu, storage, users, Windows NT event log, Windows product activation

Category	Subcategory
WMI Service Management	WMI configuration, WMI management
General	Installed applications, performance counter, security descriptor

Table 7-2. Selected WMI classes

Class	Description
CIM_DataFile	Represents a named collection of data or executable code. Currently, the provider returns files on fixed and mapped logical disks. In the future, only instances of files on local fixed disks will be returned.
Win32_BaseBoard	Represents a baseboard, which is also known as a motherboard or system board.
Win32_BIOS	Represents the attributes of the computer system's basic input/output services (BIOS) that are installed on a computer.
Win32_BootConfiguration	Represents the boot configuration of a Windows system.
Win32_CacheMemory	Represents internal and external cache memory on a computer system.
Win32_CDROMDrive	Represents a CD-ROM drive on a Windows computer system. Be aware that the name of the drive does not correspond to the logical drive letter assigned to the device.
Win32_ComputerSystem	Represents a computer system in a Windows environment.
Win32_ComputerSystem Product	Represents a product. This includes software and hardware used on this computer system.
Win32_DCOMApplication	Represents the properties of a DCOM application.

Class	Description
Win32_Desktop	Represents the common characteristics of a user's desktop. The properties of this class can be modified by the user to customize the desktop.
Win32_DesktopMonitor	Represents the type of monitor or display device attached to the computer system.
Win32_DeviceMemory Address	Represents a device memory address on a Windows system.
Win32_Directory	Represents a directory entry on a Windows computer system. A *directory* is a type of file that logically groups data files and provides path information for the grouped files. Win32_Directory does not include directories of network drives.
Win32_DiskDrive	Represents a physical disk drive as seen by a computer running the Windows operating system. Any interface to a Windows physical disk drive is a descendant (or member) of this class. The features of the disk drive seen through this object correspond to the logical and management characteristics of the drive. In some cases, this may not reflect the actual physical characteristics of the device. Any object based on another logical device would not be a member of this class.
Win32_DiskPartition	Represents the capabilities and management capacity of a partitioned area of a physical disk on a Windows system (for example, Disk #0, Partition #1).

Class	Description
Win32_DiskQuota	Tracks disk space usage for NTFS filesystem volumes. A system administrator can configure Windows to prevent further disk space use and log an event when a user exceeds a specified disk space limit. An administrator can also log an event when a user exceeds a specified disk space warning level. This class is new in Windows XP.
Win32_DMAChannel	Represents a direct memory access (DMA) channel on a Windows computer system. DMA is a method of moving data from a device to memory (or vice versa) without the help of the microprocessor. The system board uses a DMA controller to handle a fixed number of channels, each of which can be used by one (and only one) device at a time.
Win32_Environment	Represents an environment or system environment setting on a Windows computer system. Querying this class returns environment variables found in *HKLM\System\CurrentControlSet\Control \Sessionmanager\Environment* as well as *HKEY_USERS\<user sid>\Environment*.
Win32_Group	Represents data about a group account. A group account allows access privileges to be changed for a list of users (for example, Administrators).
Win32_IDEController	Manages the capabilities of an integrated device electronics (IDE) controller device.

Class	Description
Win32_IRQResource	Represents an interrupt request line (IRQ) number on a Windows computer system. An interrupt request is a signal sent to the CPU by a device or program for time-critical events. IRQ can be hardware- or software-based.
Win32_LoadOrderGroup	Represents a group of system services that define execution dependencies. The services must be initiated in the order specified by the Load Order Group, as the services are dependent on one another. These dependent services require the presence of the antecedent services to function correctly. The data in this class is derived by the provider from the registry key *System \CurrentControlSet\Control\GroupOrderList*.
Win32_LogicalDisk	Represents a data source that resolves to an actual local storage device on a Windows system.
Win32_LogonSession	Describes the logon session or sessions associated with a user logged on to Windows NT or Windows 2000.
Win32_NetworkAdapter	Represents a network adapter of a computer running on a Windows operating system.
Win32_NetworkAdapter Configuration	Represents the attributes and behaviors of a network adapter. This class includes extra properties and methods that support the management of the TCP/IP and Internetworking Packet Exchange (IPX) protocols that are independent from the network adapter.

Class	Description
WIN32_NetworkClient	Represents a network client on a Windows system. Any computer system on the network with a client relationship to the system is a descendant (or member) of this class (for example, a computer running Windows 2000 Workstation or Windows 98 that is part of a Windows 2000 domain).
Win32_NetworkConnection	Represents an active network connection in a Windows environment.
Win32_NetworkLogin Profile	Represents the network login information of a specific user on a Windows system. This includes but is not limited to password status, access privileges, disk quotas, and login directory paths.
Win32_NetworkProtocol	Represents a protocol and its network characteristics on a Win32 computer system.
Win32_NTDomain	Represents a Windows NT domain.
Win32_NTEventlogFile	Represents a logical file or directory of Windows NT events. The file is also known as the event log.
Win32_NTLogEvent	Used to translate instances from the Windows NT event log. An application must have SeSecurityPrivilege to receive events from the security event log; otherwise, "Access Denied" is returned to the application.
Win32_OnBoardDevice	Represents common adapter devices built into the motherboard (system board).

Class	Description
Win32_OperatingSystem	Represents an operating system installed on a computer running on a Windows operating system. Any operating system that can be installed on a Windows system is a descendant or member of this class. Win32_OperatingSystem is a singleton class. To get the single instance, use @ for the key. Windows Server 2003, Windows XP, Windows 2000, and Windows NT 4.0: If a computer has multiple operating systems installed, this class returns only an instance for the currently active operating system.
Win32_OSRecovery Configuration	Represents the types of information that will be gathered from memory when the operating system fails. This includes boot failures and system crashes.
Win32_PageFileSetting	Represents the settings of a page file. Information contained within objects instantiated from this class specifies the page file parameters used when the file is created at system startup. The properties in this class can be modified and deferred until startup. These settings are different from the runtime state of a page file expressed through the associated class Win32_Page FileUsage.
Win32_PageFileUsage	Represents the file used for handling virtual memory file swapping on a Win32 system. Information contained within objects instantiated from this class specifies the runtime state of the page file.
Win32_PerfRawData_Perf Net_Server	Provides raw data from performance counters that monitor communications using the WINS Server service.

Class	Description
Win32_PhysicalMemory Array	Represents details about the computer system physical memory. This includes the number of memory devices, memory capacity available, and memory type (for example, system or video memory).
Win32_PortConnector	Represents physical connection ports, such as DB-25 pin male, Centronics, or PS/2.
Win32_PortResource	Represents an I/O port on a Windows computer system.
Win32_Printer	Represents a device connected to a computer running on a Microsoft Windows operating system that can produce a printed image or text on paper or another medium.
Win32_Printer Configuration	Represents the configuration for a printer device. This includes capabilities such as resolution, color, fonts, and orientation.
Win32_PrintJob	Represents a print job generated by a Windows application. Any unit of work generated by the Print command of an application that is running on a computer running on a Windows operating system is a descendant or member of this class.
Win32_Process	Represents a process on an operating system.
Win32_Processor	Represents a device that can interpret a sequence of instructions on a computer running on a Windows operating system. On a multiprocessor computer, one instance of the Win32_Processor class exists for each processor.

Class	Description
Win32_Product	Represents products as they are installed by Windows Installer. A product generally correlates to one installation package. For information about support or requirements for installation of a specific operating system, visit the Microsoft developer documentation site (*https://aka.ms/wmi*) and search for "Operating System Availability of WMI Components."
Win32_QuickFix Engineering	Represents system-wide Quick Fix Engineering (QFE) or updates that have been applied to the current operating system.
Win32_QuotaSetting	Contains setting information for disk quotas on a volume.
Win32_Registry	Represents the system registry on a Windows computer system.

Class	Description
Win32_ScheduledJob	Represents a job created with the AT command. The Win32_ScheduledJob class does not represent a job created with the Scheduled Task Wizard from the Control Panel. You cannot change a task created by WMI in the Scheduled Tasks UI.
	Windows 2000 and Windows NT 4.0: You can use the Scheduled Tasks UI to modify the task you originally created with WMI. However, although the task is successfully modified, you can no longer access the task using WMI.
	Each job scheduled against the schedule service is stored persistently (the scheduler can start a job after a reboot) and is executed at the specified time and day of the week or month. If the computer is not active or if the scheduled service is not running at the specified job time, the schedule service runs the specified job on the next day at the specified time.
	Jobs are scheduled according to Universal Coordinated Time (UTC) with bias offset from Greenwich Mean Time (GMT), which means that a job can be specified using any time zone. The Win32_ScheduledJob class returns the local time with UTC offset when enumerating an object, and converts to local time when creating new jobs. For example, a job specified to run on a computer in Boston at 10:30 p.m. Monday PST will be scheduled to run locally at 1:30 a.m. Tuesday EST. Note that a client must take into account whether daylight saving time is in operation on the local computer, and if it is, then subtract a bias of 60 minutes from the UTC offset.

Class	Description
Win32_SCSIController	Represents a SCSI controller on a Windows system.
Win32_Service	Represents a service on a computer running on a Microsoft Windows operating system. A service application conforms to the interface rules of the Service Control Manager (SCM), and can be started by a user automatically at system start through the Services Control Panel utility or by an application that uses the service functions included in the Windows API. Services can start when there are no users logged on to the computer.
Win32_Share	Represents a shared resource on a Windows system. This may be a disk drive, printer, interprocess communication, or other shareable device.
Win32_SoftwareElement	Represents a software element, part of a software feature (a distinct subset of a product, which may contain one or more elements). Each software element is defined in a Win32_SoftwareElement instance, and the association between a feature and its Win32_Software Feature instance is defined in the Win32_SoftwareFeature SoftwareElements association class. For information about support or requirements for installation on a specific operating system, visit the Microsoft developer documentation site (*https://aka.ms/wmi*) and search for "Operating System Availability of WMI Components."

Class	Description
Win32_SoftwareFeature	Represents a distinct subset of a product that consists of one or more software elements. Each software element is defined in a Win32_SoftwareElement instance, and the association between a feature and its Win32_Software Feature instance is defined in the Win32_SoftwareFeatureSoftware Elements association class. For information about support or requirements for installation on a specific operating system, visit the Microsoft developer documentation site (*https://aka.ms/wmi*) and search for "Operating System Availability of WMI Components."
Win32_SoundDevice	Represents the properties of a sound device on a Windows computer system.
Win32_StartupCommand	Represents a command that runs automatically when a user logs on to the computer system.
Win32_SystemAccount	Represents a system account. The system account is used by the operating system and services that run under Windows NT. There are many services and processes within Windows NT that need the capability to log on internally—for example, during a Windows NT installation. The system account was designed for that purpose.
Win32_SystemDriver	Represents the system driver for a base service.
Win32_SystemEnclosure	Represents the properties that are associated with a physical system enclosure.

Class	Description
Win32_SystemSlot	Represents physical connection points, including ports, motherboard slots and peripherals, and proprietary connection points.
Win32_TapeDrive	Represents a tape drive on a Windows computer. Tape drives are primarily distinguished by the fact that they can be accessed only sequentially.
Win32_TemperatureProbe	Represents the properties of a temperature sensor (e.g., electronic thermometer).
Win32_TimeZone	Represents the time zone information for a Windows system, which includes changes required for the daylight saving time transition.
Win32_UserAccount	Contains information about a user account on a computer running on a Windows operating system. Because both the Name and Domain are key properties, enumerating Win32_User Account on a large network can affect performance negatively. Calling GetObject or querying for a specific instance has less impact.
Win32_VoltageProbe	Represents the properties of a voltage sensor (electronic voltmeter).
Win32_VolumeQuota Setting	Relates disk quota settings with a specific disk volume. Windows 2000/NT: This class is not available.
Win32_WMISetting	Contains the operational parameters for the WMI service. This class can have only one instance, which always exists for each Windows system and cannot be deleted. Additional instances cannot be created.

## CHAPTER 8

Selected COM Objects and Their Uses

As an extensibility and administration interface, many applications expose useful functionality through COM objects. Although PowerShell handles many of these tasks directly, many COM objects still provide significant value.

Table 8-1 lists a selection of the COM objects most useful to system administrators.

Table 8-1. COM identifiers and descriptions

Identifier	Description
Access.Application	Allows for interaction and automation of Microsoft Access.
Agent.Control	Allows for the control of Microsoft Agent 3D animated characters.
AutoItX3.Control	(nondefault) Provides access to Windows Automation via the AutoIt administration tool.
CEnroll.CEnroll	Provides access to certificate enrollment services.

Identifier	Description
Certificate Authority.Request	Provides access to a request to a certificate authority.
COMAdmin.COMAdminCatalog	Provides access to and management of the Windows COM+ catalog.
Excel.Application	Allows for interaction and automation of Microsoft Excel.
Excel.Sheet	Allows for interaction with Microsoft Excel worksheets.
HNetCfg.FwMgr	Provides access to the management functionality of the Windows Firewall.
HNetCfg.HNetShare	Provides access to the management functionality of Windows Connection Sharing.
HTMLFile	Allows for interaction and authoring of a new Internet Explorer document.
InfoPath.Application	Allows for interaction and automation of Microsoft InfoPath.
InternetExplorer.Application	Allows for interaction and automation of Internet Explorer.
IXSSO.Query	Allows for interaction with Microsoft Index Server.
IXSSO.Util	Provides access to utilities used along with the IXSSO.Query object.
LegitCheckControl.LegitCheck	Provide access to information about Windows Genuine Advantage status on the current computer.

Identifier	Description
MakeCab.MakeCab	Provides functionality to create and manage cabinet (*.cab*) files.
MAPI.Session	Provides access to a Messaging Application Programming Interface (MAPI) session, such as folders, messages, and the address book.
Messenger.MessengerApp	Allows for interaction and automation of Messenger.
Microsoft.FeedsManager	Allows for interaction with the Microsoft RSS feed platform.
Microsoft.ISAdm	Provides management of Microsoft Index Server.
Microsoft.Update. AutoUpdate	Provides management of the auto update schedule for Microsoft Update.
Microsoft.Update.Installer	Allows for installation of updates from Microsoft Update.
Microsoft.Update.Searcher	Provides search functionality for updates from Microsoft Update.
Microsoft.Update.Session	Provides access to local Information about Microsoft Update history.
Microsoft.Update.SystemInfo	Provides access to information related to Microsoft Update for the current system.
MMC20.Application	Allows for interaction and automation of Microsoft Management Console (MMC).
MSScriptControl. ScriptControl	Allows for the evaluation and control of WSH scripts.
Msxml2.XSLTemplate	Allows for processing of XSL transforms.

Identifier	Description
Outlook.Application	Allows for interaction and automation of your email, calendar, contacts, tasks, and more through Microsoft Outlook.
OutlookExpress.MessageList	Allows for interaction and automation of your email through Microsoft Outlook Express.
PowerPoint.Application	Allows for interaction and automation of Microsoft PowerPoint.
Publisher.Application	Allows for interaction and automation of Microsoft Publisher.
RDS.DataSpace	Provides access to proxies of Remote DataSpace business objects.
SAPI.SpVoice	Provides access to the Microsoft Speech API.
Scripting.FileSystemObject	Provides access to the computer's filesystem. Most functionality is available more directly through PowerShell or through PowerShell's support for the .NET Framework.
Scripting.Signer	Provides management of digital signatures on WSH files.
Scriptlet.TypeLib	Allows the dynamic creation of scripting type library (*.tlb*) files.
ScriptPW.Password	Allows for the masked input of plain-text passwords. When possible, you should avoid this, preferring the Read-Host cmdlet with the -AsSecureString parameter.

Identifier	Description
`SharePoint.OpenDocuments`	Allows for interaction with Microsoft SharePoint Services.
`Shell.Application`	Provides access to aspects of the Windows Explorer Shell application, such as managing windows, files and folders, and the current session.
`Shell.LocalMachine`	Provides access to information about the current machine related to the Windows shell.
`Shell.User`	Provides access to aspects of the current user's Windows session and profile.
`SQLDMO.SQLServer`	Provides access to the management functionality of Microsoft SQL Server.
`Vim.Application`	(nondefault) Allows for interaction and automation of the VIM editor.
`WIA.CommonDialog`	Provides access to image capture through the Windows Image Acquisition facilities.
`WMPlayer.OCX`	Allows for interaction and automation of Windows Media Player.
`Word.Application`	Allows for interaction and automation of Microsoft Word.
`Word.Document`	Allows for interaction with Microsoft Word documents.

Identifier	Description
WScript.Network	Provides access to aspects of a networked Windows environment, such as printers and network drives, as well as computer and domain information.
WScript.Shell	Provides access to aspects of the Windows Shell, such as applications, shortcuts, environment variables, the registry, and the operating environment.
WSHController	Allows the execution of WSH scripts on remote computers.

## CHAPTER 9

Selected Events and Their Uses

PowerShell's eventing commands give you access to events from the .NET Framework, as well as events surfaced by Windows Management Instrumentation (WMI). Table 9-1 lists a selection of .NET events. Table 9-2 lists a selection of WMI events.

Table 9-1. Selected .NET events

Type	Event	Description
System.AppDomain	AssemblyLoad	Occurs when an assembly is loaded.
System.AppDomain	TypeResolve	Occurs when the resolution of a type fails.

Type	Event	Description
System.AppDomain	ResourceResolve	Occurs when the resolution of a resource fails because the resource is not a valid linked or embedded resource in the assembly.
System.AppDomain	AssemblyResolve	Occurs when the resolution of an assembly fails.
System.AppDomain	ReflectionOnly AssemblyResolve	Occurs when the resolution of an assembly fails in the reflection-only context.
System.AppDomain	UnhandledException	Occurs when an exception is not caught.
System.Console	CancelKeyPress	Occurs when the Control modifier key (Ctrl) and C console key (C) are pressed simultaneously (Ctrl+C).
Microsoft.Win32. SystemEvents	DisplaySettings Changing	Occurs when the display settings are changing.
Microsoft.Win32. SystemEvents	DisplaySettingsChanged	Occurs when the user changes the display settings.

Type	Event	Description
Microsoft.Win32.SystemEvents	InstalledFontsChanged	Occurs when the user adds fonts to or removes fonts from the system.
Microsoft.Win32.SystemEvents	LowMemory	Occurs when the system is running out of available RAM.
Microsoft.Win32.SystemEvents	PaletteChanged	Occurs when the user switches to an application that uses a different palette.
Microsoft.Win32.SystemEvents	PowerModeChanged	Occurs when the user suspends or resumes the system.
Microsoft.Win32.SystemEvents	SessionEnded	Occurs when the user is logging off or shutting down the system.
Microsoft.Win32.SystemEvents	SessionEnding	Occurs when the user is trying to log off or shut down the system.
Microsoft.Win32.SystemEvents	SessionSwitch	Occurs when the currently logged-in user has changed.
Microsoft.Win32.SystemEvents	TimeChanged	Occurs when the user changes the time on the system clock.

Type	Event	Description
Microsoft.Win32. SystemEvents	UserPreferenceChanged	Occurs when a user preference has changed.
Microsoft.Win32. SystemEvents	UserPreferenceChanging	Occurs when a user preference is changing.
System.Net. WebClient	OpenReadCompleted	Occurs when an asynchronous operation to open a stream containing a resource completes.
System.Net. WebClient	OpenWriteCompleted	Occurs when an asynchronous operation to open a stream to write data to a resource completes.
System.Net. WebClient	DownloadString Completed	Occurs when an asynchronous resource-download operation completes.
System.Net. WebClient	DownloadDataCompleted	Occurs when an asynchronous data download operation completes.

Type	Event	Description
System.Net.WebClient	DownloadFileCompleted	Occurs when an asynchronous file download operation completes.
System.Net.WebClient	UploadStringCompleted	Occurs when an asynchronous string-upload operation completes.
System.Net.WebClient	UploadDataCompleted	Occurs when an asynchronous data-upload operation completes.
System.Net.WebClient	UploadFileCompleted	Occurs when an asynchronous file-upload operation completes.
System.Net.WebClient	UploadValuesCompleted	Occurs when an asynchronous upload of a name/value collection completes.
System.Net.WebClient	DownloadProgressChanged	Occurs when an asynchronous download operation successfully transfers some or all of the data.

Type	Event	Description
System.Net. WebClient	UploadProgressChanged	Occurs when an asynchronous upload operation successfully transfers some or all of the data.
System.Net. Sockets.Socket AsyncEventArgs	Completed	The event used to complete an asynchronous operation.
System.Net. Network Information. NetworkChange	NetworkAvailability Changed	Occurs when the availability of the network changes.
System.Net. Network Information. NetworkChange	NetworkAddressChanged	Occurs when the IP address of a network interface changes.
System.IO. FileSystemWatcher	Changed	Occurs when a file or directory in the specified path is changed.
System.IO. FileSystemWatcher	Created	Occurs when a file or directory in the specified path is created.
System.IO. FileSystemWatcher	Deleted	Occurs when a file or directory in the specified path is deleted.

Type	Event	Description
System.IO. FileSystemWatcher	Renamed	Occurs when a file or directory in the specified path is renamed.
System. Timers.Timer	Elapsed	Occurs when the interval elapses.
System. Diagnostics. EventLog	EntryWritten	Occurs when an entry is written to an event log on the local computer.
System. Diagnostics. Process	OutputDataReceived	Occurs when an application writes to its redirected StandardOutput stream.
System. Diagnostics. Process	ErrorDataReceived	Occurs when an application writes to its redirected StandardError stream.
System. Diagnostics. Process	Exited	Occurs when a process exits.
System.IO.Ports. SerialPort	ErrorReceived	Represents the method that handles the error event of a SerialPort object.

Type	Event	Description
System.IO.Ports.SerialPort	PinChanged	Represents the method that will handle the serial pin changed event of a SerialPort object.
System.IO.Ports.SerialPort	DataReceived	Represents the method that will handle the data received event of a SerialPort object.
System.Management.Automation.Job	StateChanged	Event fired when the status of the job changes, such as when the job has completed in all runspaces or failed in any one runspace.
System.Management.Automation.Debugger	DebuggerStop	Event raised when PowerShell stops execution of the script and enters the debugger as the result of encountering a breakpoint or executing a step command.

Type	Event	Description
System.Management.Automation.Debugger	BreakpointUpdated	Event raised when the breakpoint is updated, such as when it is enabled or disabled.
System.Management.Automation.Runspaces.Runspace	StateChanged	Event that is raised when the state of the runspace changes.
System.Management.Automation.Runspaces.Runspace	AvailabilityChanged	Event that is raised when the availability of the runspace changes, such as when the runspace becomes available and when it is busy.
System.Management.Automation.Runspaces.Pipeline	StateChanged	Event raised when the state of the pipeline changes.
System.Management.Automation.PowerShell	InvocationStateChanged	Event raised when the state of the pipeline of the PowerShell object changes.

Type	Event	Description
System. Management. Automation.PSData Collection[T]	DataAdded	Event that is fired after data is added to the collection.
System. Management. Automation.PSData Collection[T]	Completed	Event that is fired when the Complete method is called to indicate that no more data is to be added to the collection.
System. Management. Automation. Runspaces. RunspacePool	StateChanged	Event raised when the state of the runspace pool changes.
System. Management. Automation. Runspaces. PipelineReader[T]	DataReady	Event fired when data is added to the buffer.
System. Diagnostics. Eventing.Reader. EventLogWatcher	EventRecordWritten	Allows setting a delegate (event handler method) that gets called every time an event is published that matches the criteria specified in the event query for this object.

Type	Event	Description
System.Data. Common. DbConnection	StateChange	Occurs when the state of the event changes.
System.Data. SqlClient. SqlBulkCopy	SqlRowsCopied	Occurs every time that the number of rows specified by the Notify After property have been processed.
System.Data. SqlClient. SqlCommand	StatementCompleted	Occurs when the execution of a Transact-SQL statement completes.
System.Data. SqlClient. SqlConnection	InfoMessage	Occurs when SQL Server returns a warning or informational message.
System.Data. SqlClient. SqlConnection	StateChange	Occurs when the state of the event changes.
System.Data. SqlClient. SqlDataAdapter	RowUpdated	Occurs during Update after a command is executed against the data source. The attempt to update is made, so the event fires.

Type	Event	Description
System.Data. SqlClient. SqlDataAdapter	RowUpdating	Occurs during Update before a command is executed against the data source. The attempt to update is made, so the event fires.
System.Data. SqlClient. SqlDataAdapter	FillError	Returned when an error occurs during a fill operation.
System.Data. SqlClient. SqlDependency	OnChange	Occurs when a notification is received for any of the commands associated with this Sql Dependency object.

Generic WMI Events

Some generic WMI events include the following:

__InstanceCreationEvent

This event class generically represents the creation of instances in WMI providers, such as Processes, Services, Files, and more.

A registration for this generic event looks like:

```
$query = "SELECT * FROM __InstanceCreationEvent " +
         "WITHIN 5 " +
         "WHERE targetinstance is a
         'Win32_UserAccount'
Register-CimIndicationEvent -Query $query
```

__InstanceDeletionEvent

This event class generically represents the removal of instances in WMI providers, such as Processes, Services, Files, and more.

A registration for this generic event looks like:

```
$query = "SELECT * FROM __InstanceDeletionEvent " +
         "WITHIN 5 " +
         "WHERE targetinstance is a
         'Win32_UserAccount'
Register-CimIndicationEvent -Query $query
```

__InstanceModificationEvent

This event class generically represents the modification of instances in WMI providers, such as Processes, Services, Files, and more.

A registration for this generic event looks like:

```
$query = "SELECT * FROM __InstanceModificationEvent "
         + "WITHIN 5 " +
         "WHERE targetinstance is a
         'Win32_UserAccount'
Register-CimIndicationEvent -Query $query
```

Table 9-2. Selected WMI Events

Event	Description
Msft_WmiProvider_ OperationEvent	The Msft_WmiProvider_ OperationEvent event class is the root definition of all WMI provider events. A provider operation is defined as some execution on behalf of a client via WMI that results in one or more calls to a provider executable. The properties of this class define the identity of the provider associated with the operation being executed and is uniquely associated with instances of the class Msft_Providers. Internally, WMI can contain any number of objects that refer to a particular instance of __Win32Provider since it differentiates each object based on whether the provider supports per-user or per-locale instantiation and also depending on where the provider is being hosted. Currently TransactionIdentifier is always an empty string.
Win32_ComputerSystemEvent	This event class represents events related to a computer system.
Win32_ComputerShutdown Event	This event class represents events when a computer has begun the process of shutting down.
Win32_IP4RouteTableEvent	The Win32_IP4RouteTableEvent class represents IP route change events resulting from the addition, removal, or modification of IP routes on the computer system.

Event	Description
RegistryEvent	The registry event classes allow you to subscribe to events that involve changes in hive subtrees, keys, and specific values.
RegistryKeyChangeEvent	The RegistryKeyChangeEvent class represents changes to a specific key. The changes apply only to the key, not its subkeys.
RegistryTreeChangeEvent	The RegistryTreeChangeEvent class represents changes to a key and its subkeys.
RegistryValueChangeEvent	The RegistryValueChangeEvent class represents changes to a single value of a specific key.
Win32_SystemTrace	The SystemTrace class is the base class for all system trace events. System trace events are fired by the kernel logger via the event tracing API.
Win32_ProcessTrace	This event is the base event for process events.
Win32_ProcessStartTrace	The ProcessStartTrace event class indicates a new process has started.
Win32_ProcessStopTrace	The ProcessStopTrace event class indicates a process has terminated.
Win32_ModuleTrace	The ModuleTrace event class is the base event for module events.
Win32_ModuleLoadTrace	The ModuleLoadTrace event class indicates a process has loaded a new module.
Win32_ThreadTrace	The ThreadTrace event class is the base event for thread events.

Event	Description
Win32_ThreadStartTrace	The ThreadStartTrace event class indicates a new thread has started.
Win32_ThreadStopTrace	The ThreadStopTrace event class indicates a thread has terminated.
Win32_PowerManagement Event	The Win32_PowerManagement Event class represents power management events resulting from power state changes. These state changes are associated with either the Advanced Power Management (APM) or the Advanced Configuration and Power Interface (ACPI) system management protocols.
Win32_DeviceChangeEvent	The Win32_DeviceChangeEvent class represents device change events resulting from the addition, removal, or modification of devices on the computer system. This includes changes in the hardware configuration (docking and undocking), the hardware state, or newly mapped devices (mapping of a network drive). For example, a device has changed when a WM_DEVICECHANGE message is sent.

Event	Description
Win32_SystemConfiguration ChangeEvent	The Win32_System ConfigurationChangeEvent is an event class that indicates the device list on the system has been refreshed, meaning a device has been added or removed or the configuration changed. This event is fired when the Windows message "DevMgrRefreshOn<ComputerName>" is sent. The exact change to the device list is not contained in the message, and therefore a device refresh is required in order to obtain the current system settings. Examples of configuration changes affected are IRQ settings, COM ports, and BIOS version, to name a few.
Win32_VolumeChangeEvent	The Win32_VolumeChangeEvent class represents a local drive event resulting from the addition of a drive letter or mounted drive on the computer system (e.g., CD-ROM). Network drives are not currently supported.

## CHAPTER 10

Standard PowerShell Verbs

Cmdlets and scripts should be named using a *Verb-Noun* syntax (e.g., Get-ChildItem). The official guidance is that, with rare exception, cmdlets should use the standard PowerShell verbs. They should avoid any synonyms or concepts that can be mapped to the standard. This allows administrators to quickly understand a set of cmdlets that use a new noun.

NOTE

To quickly access this list (without the definitions), type **Get-Verb**.

Verbs should be phrased in the present tense, and nouns should be singular. Tables 10-1 through 10-6 list the different categories of standard PowerShell verbs.

Table 10-1. Standard PowerShell common verbs

Verb	Meaning	Synonyms
Add	Adds a resource to a container or attaches an element to another element	Append, Attach, Concatenate, Insert
Clear	Removes all elements from a container	Flush, Erase, Release, Unmark, Unset, Nullify
Close	Removes access to a resource	Shut, Seal
Copy	Copies a resource to another name or container	Duplicate, Clone, Replicate
Enter	Sets a resource as a context	Push, Telnet, Open
Exit	Returns to the context that was present before a new context was entered	Pop, Disconnect
Find	Searches within an unknown context for a desired item	Dig, Discover
Format	Converts an item to a specified structure or layout	Layout, Arrange
Get	Retrieves data	Read, Open, Cat, Type, Dir, Obtain, Dump, Acquire, Examine, Find, Search
Hide	Makes a display not visible	Suppress
Join	Joins a resource	Combine, Unite, Connect, Associate
Lock	Locks a resource	Restrict, Bar
Move	Moves a resource	Transfer, Name, Migrate

Verb	Meaning	Synonyms
New	Creates a new resource	Create, Generate, Build, Make, Allocate
Open	Enables access to a resource	Release, Unseal
Optimize	Increases the effectiveness of a resource	Improve, Fix
Pop	Removes an item from the top of a stack	Remove, Paste
Push	Puts an item onto the top of a stack	Put, Add, Copy
Redo	Repeats an action or reverts the action of an Undo	Repeat, Retry, Revert
Resize	Changes the size of a resource	Change, Grow, Shrink
Remove	Removes a resource from a container	Delete, Kill
Rename	Gives a resource a new name	Ren, Swap
Reset	Restores a resource to a predefined or original state	Restore, Revert
Select	Creates a subset of data from a larger data set	Pick, Grep, Filter
Search	Finds a resource (or summary information about that resource) in a collection (does not actually retrieve the resource but provides information to be used when retrieving it)	Find, Get, Grep, Select
Set	Places data	Write, Assign, Configure
Show	Retrieves, formats, and displays information	Display, Report

Verb	Meaning	Synonyms
Skip	Bypasses an element in a seek or navigation	Bypass, Jump
Split	Separates data into smaller elements	Divide, Chop, Parse
Step	Moves a process or navigation forward by one unit	Next, Iterate
Switch	Alternates the state of a resource between different alternatives or options	Toggle, Alter, Flip
Undo	Sets a resource to its previous state	Revert, Abandon
Unlock	Unlocks a resource	Free, Unrestrict
Use	Applies or associates a resource with a context	With, Having
Watch	Continually monitors an item	Monitor, Poll

Table 10-2. Standard PowerShell communication verbs

Verb	Meaning	Synonyms
Connect	Connects a source to a destination	Join, Telnet
Disconnect	Disconnects a source from a destination	Break, Logoff
Read	Acquires information from a nonconnected source	Prompt, Get
Receive	Acquires information from a connected source	Read, Accept, Peek
Send	Writes information to a connected destination	Put, Broadcast, Mail
Write	Writes information to a nonconnected destination	Puts, Print

Table 10-3. Standard PowerShell data verbs

Verb	Meaning	Synonyms
Backup	Backs up data	Save, Burn
Checkpoint	Creates a snapshot of the current state of data or its configuration	Diff, StartTransaction
Compare	Compares a resource with another resource	Diff, Bc
Compress	Reduces the size or resource usage of an item	Zip, Squeeze, Archive
Convert	Changes from one representation to another when the cmdlet supports bidirectional conversion or conversion of many data types	Change, Resize, Resample
ConvertFrom	Converts from one primary input to several supported outputs	Export, Output, Out
ConvertTo	Converts from several supported inputs to one primary output	Import, Input, In
Dismount	Detaches a name entity from a location in a namespace	Dismount, Unlink
Edit	Modifies an item in place	Change, Modify, Alter
Expand	Increases the size or resource usage of an item	Extract, Unzip
Export	Stores the primary input resource into a backing store or interchange format	Extract, Backup
Group	Combines an item with other related items	Merge, Combine, Map
Import	Creates a primary output resource from a backing store or interchange format	Load, Read

Verb	Meaning	Synonyms
Initialize	Prepares a resource for use and initializes it to a default state	Setup, Renew, Rebuild
Limit	Applies constraints to a resource	Quota, Enforce
Merge	Creates a single data instance from multiple data sets	Combine, Join
Mount	Attaches a named entity to a location in a namespace	Attach, Link
Out	Sends data to a terminal location	Print, Format, Send
Publish	Make a resource known or visible to others	Deploy, Release, Install
Restore	Restores a resource to a set of conditions that have been predefined or set by a checkpoint	Repair, Return, Fix
Save	Stores pending changes to a recoverable store	Write, Retain, Submit
Sync	Synchronizes two resources with each other	Push, Update
Unpublish	Removes a resource from public visibility	Uninstall, Revert
Update	Updates or refreshes a resource	Refresh, Renew, Index

Table 10-4. Standard PowerShell diagnostic verbs

Verb	Meaning	Synonyms
Debug	Examines a resource, diagnoses operational problems	Attach, Diagnose
Measure	Identifies resources consumed by an operation or retrieves statistics about a resource	Calculate, Determine, Analyze

Verb	Meaning	Synonyms
Ping	Determines whether a resource is active and responsive (in most instances, this should be replaced by the verb Test)	Connect, Debug
Repair	Recovers an item from a damaged or broken state	Fix, Recover, Rebuild
Resolve	Maps a shorthand representation to a more complete one	Expand, Determine
Test	Verify the validity or consistency of a resource	Diagnose, Verify, Analyze
Trace	Follow the activities of the resource	Inspect, Dig

Table 10-5. Standard PowerShell lifecycle verbs

Verb	Meaning	Synonyms
Approve	Gives approval or permission for an item or resource	Allow, Let
Assert	Declares the state of an item or fact	Verify, Check
Build	Creates an artifact (usually a binary or document) out of some set of input files (usually source code or declarative documents)	Compile, Generate
Complete	Finalizes a pending operation	Finalize, End
Confirm	Approves or acknowledges a resource or process	Check, Validate
Deny	Disapproves or disallows a resource or process	Fail, Halt
Deploy	Sends an application, website, or solution to a remote target[s] in such a way that a consumer of that solution can access it after deployment is complete	Ship, Release

Verb	Meaning	Synonyms
Disable	Configures an item to be unavailable	Halt, Hide
Enable	Configures an item to be available	Allow, Permit
Install	Places a resource in the specified location and optionally initializes it	Setup, Configure
Invoke	Calls or launches an activity that cannot be stopped	Run, Call, Perform
Register	Adds an item to a monitored or publishing resource	Record, Submit, Journal, Subscribe
Request	Submits for consideration or approval	Ask, Query
Restart	Stops an operation and starts it again	Recycle, Hup
Resume	Begins an operation after it has been suspended	Continue
Start	Begins an activity	Launch, Initiate
Stop	Discontinues an activity	Halt, End, Discontinue
Submit	Adds to a list of pending actions or sends for approval	Send, Post
Suspend	Pauses an operation, but does not discontinue it	Pause, Sleep, Break
Uninstall	Removes a resource from the specified location	Remove, Clear, Clean
Unregister	Removes an item from a monitored or publishing resource	Unsubscribe, Erase, Remove
Wait	Pauses until an expected event occurs	Sleep, Pause, Join

Table 10-6. Standard PowerShell security verbs

Verb	Meaning	Synonyms
Block	Restricts access to a resource	Prevent, Limit, Deny
Grant	Grants access to a resource	Allow, Enable
Protect	Limits access to a resource	Encrypt, Seal
Revoke	Removes access to a resource	Remove, Disable
Unblock	Removes a restriction of access to a resource	Clear, Allow
Unprotect	Removes restrictions from a protected resource	Decrypt, Decode

Index

subtraction operator, 20

A

\a escaped character, 98
\A in atomic zero-width assertions, 94
a.m./p.m. (t and tt) custom format specifiers, 116
Access.Application object, 147
AccessControl classes, 125
Active Directory, xviii, 130
Active Directory Services Interfaces (see ADSI)
Add verb, 172
Add-Member cmdlet, 55-57
Add-Type cmdlet, 55
addition (+) operator, 20
administrators, xi
ADSI (Active Directory Service Interface), xviii
Agent.Control object, 147
aliases for cmdlets, x
AliasProperty, Add-Member, 56
alternation constructs, 96
AND operator
    binary (-band), 23
    logical (-and), 22
and, XPath logical, 102
AppDomain class, 121
AppDomain event type, 153
Approve verb, 177
arbitrary variable syntax, 6
argument ($args) array, 64
arithmetic operators, 19
array cast syntax @(), 14
Array class, 121
ArrayList class, 121
arrays, 14-19
    access to array elements, 16-17
    definitions of arrays, 14-16
    hashtables, 18
    slicing of arrays, 17

-as (type conversion) operator, 26
assemblies (libraries), loading, 55
Assembly class, 121
AssemblyLoad event, 153
-AssemblyName parameter, 55
AssemblyResolve event, 154
Assert verb, 177
assignment operators, 21, 36
assignment, variable, 11-12
associative arrays, 18
atomic zero-width assertions, 94
AutoItX3.Control object, 147
Automation.Job event type, 160
AvailabilityChanged event, 161

B

\B in atomic zero-width assertions, 95
\b
    in atomic zero-width assertions, 94
    escaped character, 98
background (&) operator, 61
backreference constructs, 96
Backup verb, 175
base classes and interfaces, 46
begin statement, 71
BigInt class, 14
binary numbers, 13
binary operators, 23-25, 27, 28
BinaryReader class, 123
BinaryWriter class, 123
Bitmap class, 126
block comments, 3
Block verb, 179
Booleans, 8
break keyword, 75
break statement, 42
BreakpointUpdated event, 160
BufferedStream class, 123
Build verb, 177

About the Author

Lee Holmes is a security architect in Azure Security, an original developer on the PowerShell team, and has been an authoritative source of information about PowerShell since its earliest betas. His vast experience with both world-scale security and operational management—and PowerShell itself—give him the background to integrate both the "how" and the "why" into discussions.

You can find him on Twitter (*@Lee_Holmes*), as well as his personal site (*https://www.leeholmes.com*).

Colophon

The animal on the cover of *PowerShell Pocket Reference* is an eastern box turtle (*Terrapene carolina carolina*). This box turtle is native to North America, specifically northern parts of the United States and Mexico. The male turtle averages about six inches long and has red eyes; the female is a bit smaller and has yellow eyes.

This turtle is omnivorous as a youth but largely herbivorous as an adult. Its domed shell is hinged on the bottom and snaps tightly shut if the turtle is in danger. Box turtles usually stay within the area in which they are born, rarely leaving a 750-foot radius. When mating, male turtles sometimes shove and push one another to win a female's attention. During copulation, it is possible for the male turtle to fall backward, be unable to right himself, and starve to death.

Although box turtles can live for more than 100 years, their habitats are seriously threatened by land development and roads. Turtles need loose, moist soil in which to lay eggs and burrow during their long hibernation season. Experts strongly discourage taking turtles from their native habitats—not only will it disrupt the community's breeding opportunities, but turtles become extremely stressed outside of their known habitats and may perish quickly.

Many of the animals on O'Reilly covers are endangered; all of them are important to the world.

Color illustration by Karen Montgomery, based on a black and white engraving from Dover's *Animals*. The cover fonts are Gilroy Semibold and Guardian Sans. The text font is Adobe Minion Pro; the heading font is Adobe Myriad Condensed; and the code font is Dalton Maag's Ubuntu Mono.